A Search for Institutional Distinctiveness

Barbara K. Townsend, *Editor*
Loyola University of Chicago

NEW DIRECTIONS FOR COMMUNITY COLLEGES
ARTHUR M. COHEN, *Editor-in-Chief*
FLORENCE B. BRAWER, *Associate Editor*

Number 65, Spring 1989

Paperback sourcebooks in
The Jossey-Bass Higher Education Series

Jossey-Bass Inc., Publishers
San Francisco • London

Barbara K. Townsend (ed.).
A Search for Institutional Distinctiveness.
New Directions for Community Colleges, no. 65.
Volume XVII, number 1.
San Francisco: Jossey-Bass, 1989.

New Directions for Community Colleges
Arthur M. Cohen, *Editor-in-Chief;* Florence B. Brawer, *Associate Editor*

New Directions for Community Colleges is published quarterly
by Jossey-Bass Inc., Publishers (publication number USPS 121-710),
in association with the ERIC Clearinghouse for Junior Colleges.
New Directions is numbered sequentially—please order extra copies
by sequential number. The volume and issue numbers above are
included for the convenience of libraries. Second-class postage paid
at San Francisco, California, and at additional mailing offices.
POSTMASTER: Send address changes to Jossey-Bass, Inc., Publishers,
350 Sansome Street, San Francisco, California 94104.

The material in this publication is based on work sponsored wholly
or in part by the Office of Educational Research and Improvement,
U.S. Department of Education, under contract number RI-88-062002.
Its contents do not necessarily reflect the views of the Department,
or any other agency of the U.S. Government.

Editorial correspondence should be sent to the Editor-in-Chief, Arthur
M. Cohen, at the ERIC Clearinghouse for Junior Colleges, University
of California, Los Angeles, California 90024.

Library of Congress Catalog Card Number LC 85-644753

International Standard Serial Number ISSN 0194-3081

International Standard Book Number ISBN 1-55542-862-2

Cover art by WILLI BAUM

Manufactured in the United States of America. Printed on acid-free paper.

Ordering Information

The paperback sourcebooks listed below are published quarterly and can be ordered either by subscription or single copy.
Subscriptions cost $60.00 per year for institutions, agencies, and libraries. Individuals can subscribe at the special rate of $45.00 per year *if payment is by personal check.* (Note that the full rate of $60.00 applies if payment is by institutional check, even if the subscription is designated for an individual.) Standing orders are accepted.
Single copies are available at $14.95 when payment accompanies order. (California, New Jersey, New York, and Washington, D.C., residents please include appropriate sales tax.) For billed orders, cost per copy is $14.95 plus postage and handling.
Substantial discounts are offered to organizations and individuals wishing to purchase bulk quantities of Jossey-Bass sourcebooks. Please inquire.
Please note that these prices are for the calendar year 1989 and are subject to change without notice. Also, some titles may be out of print and therefore not available for sale.
To ensure correct and prompt delivery, all orders must give either the *name of an individual* or an *official purchase order number.* Please submit your order as follows:

Subscriptions: specify series and year subscription is to begin.
Single Copies: specify sourcebook code (such as, CC1) and first two words of title.

Mail orders for United States and Possessions, Latin America, Canada, Japan, Australia, and New Zealand to:
Jossey-Bass Inc., Publishers
350 Sansome Street
San Francisco, California 94104

Mail orders for all other parts of the world to:
Jossey-Bass Limited
28 Banner Street
London EC1Y 8QE

New Directions for Community Colleges Series
Arthur M. Cohen, *Editor-in-Chief*
Florence B. Brawer, *Associate Editor*

CC1   *Toward a Professional Faculty,* Arthur M. Cohen
CC2   *Meeting the Financial Crisis,* John Lombardi
CC3   *Understanding Diverse Students,* Dorothy M. Knoell

Contents

Editor's Notes

Certain higher education institutions are so well known that the mention of their names immediately evokes a distinctive image. When Harvard is mentioned, for example, most of us think of ivy-covered buildings filled with the brightest and best students, many of whom come from "old money" and most of whom will achieve prominence in their chosen careers. But, while Harvard has a distinctive national image, most community colleges do not. They have high visibility within their local region and some visibility within their state but virtually no name recognition nationally. Yet this positive recognition on a smaller scale is what helps ensure a community college's success.

Seeking out and maintaining this positive local and statewide recognition, then, is a primary concern of community college leaders. How do they develop a positive institutional image among external constituents? In the literature dealing with development of institutional image, the usual emphasis is on means rather than substance. Ways to project a positive image are detailed while the question of whether the positive image reflects the reality of the institution is rarely raised.

In contrast to the usual approaches to institutional image, this sourcebook emphasizes institutional substance and reality. Implicit in a knowledge of institutional reality is the process of evaluation—determining an institution's strengths and limitations in order to understand its potential for distinctiveness. Conducting a search for institutional distinctiveness along the lines suggested in this sourcebook is a form of evaluation. The search shows a college's leaders the dimensions on which the college is distinctive as an educational institution and those on which it is not; the leaders can then determine whether the institution's existing distinctive dimensions are important or if more substantive ones should be sought. The ultimate result will be a more distinctive institution, one whose external image matches the internal reality.

Both the relationship between institutional distinctiveness and image and the concept of institutional distinctiveness itself are examined in the first three chapters. In Chapter One, Daniel Savage discusses current widely held images of the community college and suggests that the institution, as an educational type, can achieve a distinctive image of quality within the overarching image of "comprehensive community college." Specific examples of distinctive programs, services, and delivery systems in community colleges across the country are provided in Chapter Two, where Joseph Hankin describes the results of his national search for these institutional elements. In Chapter Three, I present the concept of

1

2

institutional distinctiveness that underlies this sourcebook. In addition, I provide an overview of the process by which those within a community college can research their institution's distinctive elements and features.

Chapters Four through Seven detail the specifics of how to conduct a search for institutional distinctiveness and what to do with the results of the search. Michael Quanty, in Chapter Four, describes two ways to start the search—either by establishing a college committee or selecting a consultant—and ways to proceed in either instance. Since the committee or consultant will be conducting research about the institution, Chapter Five follows with James Ratcliff's proposals for data collection, analysis, and verification through such activities as institutional histories, needs assessments, and institutional impact studies. In Chapter Six, Robert Templin links use of the data derived from the research to strategic planning and to the college's particular stage of organizational development. In Chapter Seven, I enumerate some specific institutional benefits that can be derived from the various stages of the search.

To show that theory can be translated into practice, James Catanzaro and I present a case study in Chapter Eight of one institution's search for institutional distinctiveness. The chapter includes the findings of Triton College's search and suggestions that Triton might follow to achieve a more distinctive image. The concluding chapter cites recent publications drawn from the ERIC data base on other ways in which individual community colleges can ascertain their strengths and limitations.

Institutional leaders who elect to evaluate their institutions by the means described in this sourcebook are making a commitment to institutional excellence and to the creation of an institution worthy of a distinctive image.

Barbara K. Townsend
Editor

Barbara K. Townsend is assistant professor of higher education at Loyola University of Chicago and is a former community college faculty member and administrator.

*While the community college's policy of open admissions often
seems incompatible with public perceptions of educational
quality, these colleges can build on their dominant image of
being comprehensive to project a distinctive image of quality
in the twenty-first century.*

Images of Community Colleges for the Twenty-First Century

Daniel D. Savage

In 1968 a community college was built in my hometown of Willoughby,
Ohio. One year before that, I, like half the other high school seniors in
Willoughby, had been preparing to select a college. At that time, a favor-
ite saying about the most popular local college choice, Kent State University, was, "If you can't go to college, go to Kent." Now, twenty years
after Lakeland Community College opened its doors in Willoughby, the
catchy saying about Kent has been replaced with, "If you can't go to
college, go to Lakeland."

This saying typifies the attitude many high school students across
the country have about the academically and financially accessible community college serving their high school area. Because the community
college is known for its open-admissions policy, the institution is often
perceived to be of poor quality—that is, not a real college. Evidence of
this attitude is provided by a recent survey of students conducted by
Lakeland's educational marketing department (Wright, 1986). According
to the survey results, students' perception of the quality of Ohio's postsecondary institutions corresponded nearly exactly to the selectivity of
the college or university's admissions criteria: The more selective the
institution, the greater its quality was perceived to be.

B. K. Townsend (ed.). *A Search for Institutional Distinctiveness.*
New Directions for Community Colleges, no. 65. San Francisco: Jossey-Bass, Spring 1989.

Comparing Student Profiles

What people fail to realize is that there is a great variation among community colleges in the abilities and achievements of their entering students. Overall, however, the student profile in community colleges closely resembles that of the "open-admissions" high schools they serve as well as that of college-going students in general. An examination of a longitudinal study of the 1980 high school sophomore and senior cohort groups (Center for Educational Statistics, 1986) provides evidence for this statement. For the 1980 high school sophomore cohort, community colleges enrolled 25.5 percent of all students who attended postsecondary institutions full time in the academic year 1982–83. Four-year colleges and universities enrolled 62 percent while "other schools" enrolled the remaining 12.5 percent. Table 1 indicates the academic ability and socioeconomic status (SES) of these students.

Several observations can be made from the data shown in Table 1. First of all, community colleges enroll a disproportionate number of students from the bottom three ability quartiles as well as the bottom three SES quartiles as compared with four-year schools. The difference, however, between the two institutional types is not as severe as one might expect. While students in the highest ability quartile are clearly underrepresented in the community college, it is significant to observe that among the full-time students enrolled in college immediately following high school graduation, 14.1 percent of the "high ability" *are* in community colleges. Since community colleges are only enrolling 25.5 percent of all full-time students, the 14.1 percent of the "high ability" group repre-

Table 1. Profile of Full-Time Student Enrollment, 1982–83, Sophomore Cohort

	Four-Year Colleges	Two-Year Colleges	Other Schools
All college students	62.0	25.5	12.5
Ability level			
Low	30.8	38.0	31.2
Med/low	36.9	38.5	24.6
Med/high	55.5	31.9	12.6
High	81.4	14.1	4.5
Socioeconomic status			
Lowest quartile	44.1	30.4	25.5
Med/low	49.3	31.5	19.2
Med/high	59.5	28.4	12.1
High	76.3	18.5	5.2

Source: Center for Education Statistics, 1986.

sents a significant share. Moreover, community colleges enroll a disproportionate share of "med/high ability" students. Four-year schools are overrepresented only in the "high ability" quartile.

On the other side of the coin, four-year colleges, many of which employ more selective admissions criteria than do community colleges, enroll 30.8 percent of the "low ability" college students. This would indicate that four-year schools, in aggregate, face a similar magnitude of remedial education needs as community colleges do.

From the standpoint of socioeconomic status, four-year schools enroll an elite of the "high SES" students, enrolling 76.3 percent of all students in this category. Four-year schools are underrepresented in the three other SES quartiles. On the other hand, community colleges enroll only 18.5 percent of the "high SES" group and are overrepresented in the lower SES quartiles. Community colleges continue, it is clear, to bear the responsibility for social and economic mobility for Americans.

Looking at Elitism and Quality

While the current hierarchy of higher education institutions clearly delivers a disproportionate share of the most academically able students to the four-year college sector, it is not evident that this hierarchical system promises the most social good, for a variety of reasons. To begin with, how well founded is the belief that quality and limited access are interrelated? Without rehearsing what is undoubtedly a lengthy argument regarding the value of elitism in promoting student learning, let us make some general propositions.

First, elitism may promote the learning outcomes for the lucky ones who are selected, but America is not willing to pay the cost of that elitism in terms of denied opportunity. Even former Secretary of Education William Bennett agrees with the popular notion that a first-rate education is the birthright of all Americans. When asked about the role of special programs for the "gifted and talented," Bennett (1986) replied that all students should get the curriculum offered to the select few.

Second, it is not at all clear that elitist education is effective, even in the education of the select. While a disproportionate share of Harvard, Stanford, and Wharton MBAs may be running America's largest corporations—where family ties and inherited wealth can significantly advance one's chances of climbing to the top—many successful entrepreneurs have a very different educational background, which may include the community college. For example, Ross Perot, perhaps America's best-known entrepreneur, is a graduate of a Texas community college.

Third, all elitist educational systems rely heavily on a set of performance measurements for admissions. In most societies, these measurements are taken in the teen years. The size and nature of the society's educational investment in the individual is based on performance measures available at that time. Yet these performance measures can be highly unpredictable indicators of human potential. The list of human geniuses who have been or would have been overlooked by such screening measures is long and distinguished.

Thus, the earlier the "cutoff date," the greater is the parental influence (versus that of teachers and peers) on the student's choice of college. While parental influence is not necessarily negative, elitist systems with early cutoff dates minimize the effect of the educational system in obviating class barriers. Parental educational attainment and socioeconomic status become "inherited" or "learned" characteristics to an even greater degree in elitist systems.

Fourth, the greatest experiment in access in the history of American education—the development of the publicly funded secondary school system—has clearly demonstrated the ability of "open-access" schools to graduate students who will perform in society's highest roles. Initially, the founding of these schools was met by much skepticism regarding their ability to "prep" students for entrance into America's leading private universities. For those with sufficient means, the public high school was hardly an alternative to the New England preparatory school. Yet, by the end of the 1960s, an ever-increasing majority of students at America's most selective colleges and universities were graduates of public schools.

Changing the Public Perception of the Community College

Assuming, then, that the public perceptions that automatically link elitist or selective schools with high quality, and unselective or open-admissions schools with low quality, are fallacious, the question becomes: How do we change these perceptions? First of all, negative stereotypes regarding the educational quality of community colleges will probably fade in time. As educational institutions, community colleges are still extremely young: Their median age is only twenty-four years (American Association of Community and Junior Colleges, 1987). As a generation of Americans experiences these colleges either as students or parents of students, attitudes toward the quality of their programs are likely to improve. Also, the concept of open access in higher education is a relatively new one. Community colleges, like public secondary schools before them, will over time build greater understanding of their ability to provide first-rate learning experiences to a population that represents the full spectrum of abilities.

While negative stereotypes associated with their open access should fade in time, community colleges face significant decisions that will enhance or detract from the desired overall image of their educational quality. Community college leaders select, both consciously and unconsciously, from a variety of institutional images when they make decisions regarding the future of their institution. Selection of these images may enhance or confound prior public perceptions. Institutional leaders must be conscious of the many varied and often contradictory images available for community colleges and of the many channels for communicating these images.

Fostering an Image of Comprehensiveness

Using her taxonomy of "Preferred Institutional Directions," Townsend (1986) found overwhelming support for the direction or concept of "comprehensive community college" among community college administrators and faculty in the State University of New York community college system. Eighty percent of the administrators and 77 percent of the faculty who responded to her survey preferred this direction for the community college in comparison to the other three directions of "academically oriented two-year college" (16 and 19 percent), "community-based learning center" (4 and 2 percent), and "postsecondary occupational training center" (0 and 0.5 percent).

Reflecting a similar attraction to the notion of comprehensiveness, the National Council for Marketing and Public Relations selected as its recent theme for National Community College Month, "Where America Goes to College." More specific occupational or academic themes were rejected in favor of this broader image.

If the image of a comprehensive, community-centered institution is popular with and accepted by the institution's faculty and administrators as well as by outside groups, community college leaders face two important questions. First of all, what specific institutional features or elements can enhance or detract from that image? Second, how can the image of a comprehensive, community-centered institution be effectively communicated to the community itself?

Several distinct and important institutional features are implied in the concept of the "comprehensive community college." "Comprehensive" implies a range of programs, both technical and academic; a variety of services; and no exclusion of important programs. "Community" implies the serving of local needs, local control and "ownership," and participation and involvement of community members. "College" implies an educational level beyond high school, an academic challenge, training for professions, transferability of academic credits, and a community of scholars. These features are by no means exhaustive, but they are ways in which the comprehensive community college image can be manifested.

Community college trustees, administrators, faculty and students who are concerned with developing a positive, distinctive institutional image need to be aware of the wide range of possible institutional features that can affect the perception of a "comprehensive community college." Figure 1 delineates some of these features and whether they contribute to positive or negative images of the comprehensive community college. While each feature's impact on institutional image is only speculative, research in this area could yield important information for image planners.

As Figure 1 indicates, the concept of the comprehensive community college has great potential for generating a distinctive institutional image in the twenty-first century. Community college leaders need to be aware, however, that the inclusion of technical programs to provide a compre-

Figure 1. The Effect of Specific Institutional Features on the Image of a Comprehensive Community College

Positive Image	Negative Image
Comprehensive	
1. Has comprehensive curriculum	Has few programs
2. Has transfer programs, both academic and technical	Has vocational-technical programs only or has terminal programs only
Community	
1. Has central role in community	Has peripheral role
2. Has close working ties and cooperative programs with secondary schools	Has infrequent contact with those in secondary schools
3. Has high visibility in the community	Has low visibility
4. Meets community educational needs	Is indifferent to community needs
5. Is open to all	Is open to select few
6. Serves broad range of ages	Serves only traditional student age group
7. Has strong role in community economic development	Has minimal role in economic development
8. Has active program advisory groups	Has inactive advisory groups
9. Has well-functioning college foundation	Has no foundation or limited citizen involvement
10. Has close ties with community employers	Has weak ties with employers
College	
1. Has rigorous academic and technical programs	Offers recreational courses such as "belly dancing"
2. Has college marketing and public relations coordinated to reinforce collegiate image	Lacks cohesive goals and strategies in its public relations and college marketing
3. Has college publications that enhance collegiate identity	Projects noncollegiate images in publications

hensive academic curriculum holds perils for a positive institutional image. The genius of America's community college system is that it incorporated under one roof technical education and transfer education. Unfortunately, technical education has also been labeled "terminal" education, thus creating an image trap. America's young people—and their parents as well—want to keep their options for the future open. To the extent that terminal vocational programs are viewed as an irrevocable decision from which there is no turning back, they will be shunned by those who still want or have a variety of options. The image trap of terminal vocational programs may explain the hesitancy of many students to take advantage of excellent vocational programs at the secondary school level. While the primary goal of technical education is to prepare students for immediate employment (in comparison to transfer education, whose primary goal is to prepare students for junior standing in a four-year college or university), this goal does not necessarily imply that technical education must be "terminal." Instead of a rigid division between these two areas of a comprehensive curriculum, institutions need creative efforts and development of curriculum that can serve students with a variety of educational aspirations, aspirations that may change over time. While not all students need to or should progress to the baccalaureate level of education, the critical factor is that the individual should not be tracked into a path from which there is no return. The student should be able to choose options that make sense in the short run yet leave open the possibility for further growth in the long run.

This catalogue of institutional features and possible images associated with them, while not complete, suggests that college leaders need to be aware of how decisions about institutional features either support or detract from intended images. For example, Dale Parnell (1982) has warned community college leaders that the continuing education component, though peripheral to the academic program, might have a strong negative influence on the public perception of the college's academic program. In a related vein, the Commission on the Future of Community Colleges (1988) recommends that continuing education courses "reflect both community needs and the educational traditions of the institution."

Some community colleges such as Miami–Dade have already earned images as colleges of distinction. Over time, more community colleges will distinguish themselves in their communities and states, but doing so will require conscious efforts on the part of institutional leaders to build a consistent image of quality.

References

American Association of Community and Junior Colleges. *AACJC Fall 1987 College Survey.* Unpublished data. Washington, D.C.: American Association of Community and Junior Colleges, 1987.

Bennett, W. "First Lessons: A Report on Elementary Education." Speech presented to the National Press Club, Washington, D.C., September 2, 1986.

Center for Educational Statistics. *High School and Beyond.* Computerized Data Files. Washington, D.C.: Center for Educational Statistics, U.S. Department of Education, 1986.

Commission on the Future of Community Colleges. *Building Communities: A Vision for a New Century.* Washington, D.C.: American Association of Community and Junior Colleges, 1988.

Parnell, D. "Will Belly Dancing Be Our Nemesis?" *Community College Catalyst,* 1982, *12* (3), 4-5.

Townsend, B. "Preferred Directions and Images for the Community College: A View from Inside." *Research in Higher Education,* 1986, *25* (5), 316-327.

Wright, T. *Survey of Attitudes of High School Seniors Toward Postsecondary Institutions.* Mentor, Ohio: Department of Educational Marketing, Lakeland Community College, 1986.

Daniel D. Savage is editor and publisher of Community College Week.

Examples of distinctive community college programs,
services, and delivery systems indicate just how distinctive
these educational institutions are.

What Makes the Community College Distinctive

Joseph N. Hankin

Community colleges are distinctive from other higher education institutions on many dimensions, including their historical development, philosophy, student body, faculty, organization, facilities, finances, community relations, programs, services, and delivery systems. This chapter briefly discusses many of these features; then it concentrates on examples of programs, services, and delivery systems that have made specific institutions distinctive.

Unique Features of Community Colleges

A number of authors have examined the growth of the community college as an educational institution. Both Vaughan (1985) and Brick (1963) have brilliantly traced the historical development, philosophy, and mission of the community and junior college movement in America. Brick asked to "what manner of child" the movement had given birth and, in telling the tale, painted a picture of a unique institution.

How distinctive the two-year college had become was chronicled by Fields (1962) as he posited the theory that community and junior colleges, unlike other institutions of higher education in the United States, were democratic, comprehensive, community oriented, dedicated to lifelong

B. K. Townsend (ed.). *A Search for Institutional Distinctiveness.*
New Directions for Community Colleges, no. 65. San Francisco: Jossey-Bass, Spring 1989.

education, and adaptable. Fields wrote, "Community colleges are like other colleges in some respects; . . . But there are real differences. . . . These differences are all indications of the efforts that community colleges are making to adapt to the problems posed, the students enrolled, and the communities served" (p. 43). Fields then used case studies of several institutions to make the point that community and junior colleges were distinctive with regard to curricular range, admissions requirements, heterogeneity of students, and other factors.

The community college's problems with role definition and focus have been traced in several works. Clark (1960), in his classic work on the "open-door college," concluded that the multiplicity of roles displayed in institutions of this type blurred the sharpness of their educational focus. In another early work, Blocker, Plummer, and Richardson (1965) described the internal struggle in two-year institutions to develop their characteristic profile. The authors concluded that too many colleges were devoting too many resources to the transfer function and not enough to the technical programs that made them special. More recently, Roueche and Baker (1987) have described Miami–Dade Community College in Florida both as a distinctive institution and as one that has worked out its identity problems and has become an example for institutions of its type.

Warren (1985) has traced the changing characteristics of community college students and clearly demonstrated the differences between students at two-year institutions and other types of colleges with regard to sex, age, full-time versus part-time status, racial and ethnic group membership, academic ability, social class, and educational purpose, for example.

Just as the students are different, so too are the faculty in comparison to their colleagues at four-year colleges. For instance, Cohen (1988) has found community college faculty more typically to have the master's degree as the highest earned, less apt to be members of academic disciplinary organizations, and more apt to be unionized. Certainly community college faculty's salary and tenure rates differ from those of their counterparts in four-year colleges and universities, according to the latest annual AAUP survey (American Association of University Professors, 1988).

Interestingly, few, if any, studies of the differences among institutions of higher education with regard to organization or facilities have been completed. It stands to reason that the organization of many two-year colleges that are smaller than their four-year counterparts would have fewer vice-presidents and provosts. There are many two-year colleges, however, that are larger than four-year institutions (the average size of two-year colleges is greater in enrollment than the average size of four-year colleges). Moreover, the greater prominence of functions such as community services in two-year colleges would seem to dictate a different organizational structure.

Similarly, the physical plants of two-year institutions differ from those of their four-year counterparts. Many fewer two-year colleges have dormitories by nature of the mission of the public institutions. Again, it stands to reason that two-year colleges, because they are younger in age on the average, would have newer physical plants, but, once again, there has been no definitive study to cite.

When we turn to finances, however, we do have national data (Stern and Chandler, 1987) to demonstrate that two-year colleges, in comparison to their sister four-year institutions, spend less per student, spend a higher proportion on instruction, receive their revenues in differing proportions from their sources, and attract different and less financial aid.

The dimension of "community relations" differs according to college and location, but, for the most part, community colleges, which try to relate to their local communities as part of their normal functions, may be said to place more emphasis on this activity than four-year institutions do.

Exemplary Programs, Services, and Delivery Systems

It is with regard to programs, services, and delivery systems, however, that the two-year community and junior colleges more precisely establish their distinctiveness, not only from four-year colleges but even from one another. Again, if one looks to the early literature, such as the works by Fields (1962) and Brick (1963), community colleges are not supposed to resemble one another but are supposed to reflect the needs of their various communities. To the extent that they do so, they fulfill their unique missions.

In January 1988, I wrote to each of the state directors of community colleges throughout the United States to elicit nominations of what they considered to be the one or two most distinctive two-year college programs in their respective states. Based on the responses of twenty-two directors, the results are reported here alphabetically in order to avoid the necessity of ranking them in any other way.

Alaska: Prince William Sound Community College. The only community college in Alaska that has not been absorbed into one of the three state universities as an extension program, this college serves sixteen separate communities with a total population of less than 20,000 individuals spread over 45,000 square miles. Some of its students live in communities only accessible by air or water. To reach these students, Prince William utilizes computer-assisted instruction, videotapes, and teleconferencing techniques. Its Developmental Disabilities Program, unique in Alaska, provides training for paraprofessionals working with handicapped individuals.

The site of the main campus is Valdez, the southern end of the trans-Alaska pipeline and a port from which 25 percent of U.S. crude oil is shipped. It is not surprising, therefore, to find the college involved in both local and statewide economic development: Specifically, it has entered into an agreement with the Alaska Pacific Refining Company to provide training for local residents for employment at the $700 million refinery that is being constructed. The president of the college also serves as the mayor of Valdez.

Arizona: Central Arizona College. This college's Flight Nurse Training Program was established to meet the expressed job-training needs of Samaritan Health Services, which operates Samaritan Air Evac, one of the leading flight emergency medical air services in the nation. Other emergency medical service flight programs developed have been Maternal Nurse Transport, Neonatal Nurse Transport, Flight Respiratory Therapy, and Flight Paramedic Training. This college, again alert to local needs, has also developed a certificate program in recreational vehicle (RV) maintenance and repair to meet the rapidly growing RV sales and service industry in the state.

Colorado: Aims Community College. Aims's Biofeedback Program is reputed to be the only two-year college program in the nation that also serves as a basic requirement for a master's degree at a state university (the University of Northern Colorado). Aims also has one of three Pilot Entry Programs in the nation (Miami–Dade in Florida and San Jacinto in Texas share the distinction). This program takes nonpilots and trains them in two years to be ready to fly as commercial airline copilots.

Florida: Several Community Colleges. According to the Florida State Board of Community Colleges, Florida Association of Community Colleges, and Florida Department of Education (n.d.), Central Florida Community College has one of six Microdyne Automated Terminal Satellite Downlink installations in the nation; it provides programming and services for business and health care agencies, such as teleconferencing, corporate training and seminars, and special business-governmental-news programming. Florida Keys Community College is the exclusive provider of commercial diving safety training for the U.S. Army Corps of Engineers. Lake City Community College has served for more than four decades as a statewide center for the training of forest technicians. Pensacola Junior College helps blind and otherwise visually impaired students prepare for life through its Skill Center for Independent Living. Seminole Community College has increased the number of volunteer tutors working with literacy students through its Project Literacy United States (PLUS).

Hawaii: Honolulu Community College. Since Hawaii is a state that has one of the largest proportions of women in the work force, a need for high-quality child care is obvious. This college has developed a program to train professional nannies to provide in the home ongoing full-time child care for infants to preschool-age children.

Illinois: Danville Area Community College. A few years ago, this institution, which has helped its community in economic development for years, recognized a major community problem: poor management-labor relations. The college was instrumental in hosting the Symposium of Labor-Management Cooperation, which brought together for the first time all of the area's key figures in labor and management. As a result, the Danville Area Labor-Management Council was formed with the college's president serving as its chair. In its six years of existence, the council has helped to start successful labor-management committees at two major firms; attracted a new medium-security prison to the area, representing $37.5 million of construction and more than 450 new jobs (twenty-two other Illinois communities were in the competition); and kept businesses in the area as well as attracted new firms.

Iowa: North Iowa Area Community College. The North Iowa Area Community College–Saint Joseph Mercy Hospital Consortium is an arrangement between a regional hospital, which manages eight hospitals in surrounding communities, and the community college, which serves nine counties. The two institutions work together to provide a comprehensive health occupations program, including continuing health education, and to staff a regional health education center for the merged area they serve. By pooling staff, the two institutions can offer lower-cost programs to those who participate.

Kentucky: University of Kentucky Community College System. The Mobile Dental Hygiene Program consists of three elements: a permanently located unit at Lexington Technical Institute and two mobile programs, one serving the western and the other the eastern portion of the state. Each of the mobile programs is located at one college for three years before being rotated to another college in the region. Thus, the programs have been offered at Ashland (two cycles), Somerset, Paducah, Hazard, and Madisonville community colleges and are currently being offered at Maysville and Southeast community colleges. Kentucky, like other states, suffers from an uneven distribution of allied health professionals, especially in rural areas. This program solves a public-policy need in addition to providing a cost-efficient way of spreading scarce resources around the state.

Louisiana: Southern University, Shreveport-Bossier City. Founded in 1967, this institution has a student body that is 90 percent black and a faculty and administrative staff that is 75 percent minority. The location of its downtown campus has made it a natural training site for small-business minority entrepreneurs and businesspeople, and the geographical location of the college makes it a health care instructional center for parts of three states: Arkansas, Louisiana, and Texas.

Maryland: Several Community Colleges. According to the Maryland State Board for Community Colleges (1987a, 1987b), several of its colleges have innovative programs. The Center for Study of Local Issues at Anne Arundel Community College offers students an opportunity to gain field experience in research methodologies (for example, on the natural waterways of Annapolis, the state capital) and helps reinforce the college's role as a major resource in the intellectual life of the community. Cecil Community College has the only equine apprenticeship program in the nation under the Federal Bureau of Apprenticeship and Training. Garrett Community College has a statewide program in wildlife/fisheries management that capitalizes on the variety of ecological resources in the western part of the state. More than 60 percent of the faculty members at Hagerstown Junior College have returned to the business, industry, or agency of their initial expertise under a college-sponsored program designed to combat employee burnout and to refresh specialty skills. In addition to a nationally acclaimed adult basic education program, Harford Community College has a series of programs jointly sponsored with the local board of education designed to certify public school teachers in mathematics, train them in science, and give instruction in the use of microcomputers.

Massachusetts: Bunker Hill Community College. This college is dedicated to the concept that members of the college community must understand and be able to function in cultures other than their own. To further this objective, the college has faculty exchange programs, a program of visiting scholars, and student exchange programs with three European institutions (the Lycée René Cassin in Strasbourg, France; Blackpool and Flyde colleges in Blackpool, England; and the Thames Polytechnic Institute in London). In addition, there are study-travel abroad programs; the Central American Scholarship Program, which, in conjunction with eleven other community colleges across the nation, awards Peace Scholarships to deserving Central American students from disadvantaged backgrounds; and a cooperative arrangement with nearby Tufts University, which provides workshops for teams of elementary and middle school teachers, giving them resources with which to introduce the theme "The Common Humanity of Peoples" into their classrooms and those of others.

Michigan: Kellogg Community College. A new electronic delivery system, the Education Utility, is being tried out by the college, local public schools, a library, and a museum with the help of a grant from the Kellogg Foundation. Its objectives are to encourage the development of self-directedness in goal setting, learning, and the development of lifetime learning skills. Thus far, the Job Information Network, housed in the public library, is used by all as a referral and research service for career change considerations. The next step is to develop mutual use of data bases and software. Ultimately what will develop is an educational maintenance organization, similar to the health maintenance organizations (HMOs) so prevalent today in the health care industry, in which each agency will get more out of the collaborative endeavor than it contributes alone.

Minnesota: The Minnesota Community Colleges. Working together, the community colleges in the state have mounted two programs worthy of note here. The first is the Alliss Opportunity Grant Program, which encourages adults who are over twenty-five, who have been out of high school or college for at least seven years, and who do not have a college degree to return to education by offering them a free college course. To date, over 17,000 residents of Minnesota have taken advantage of this program by attending classes in one of the eighteen local community colleges. These students, on the average, have done better than B work and often continue to take other courses toward a degree. In addition, the state has encouraged high school juniors and seniors to take college courses at no cost. Because of their locations throughout the state, the community colleges have educated the majority of students taking advantage of this Postsecondary Enrollment Options Program.

New York: LaGuardia Community College. Middle College High School was established as an alternative high school program by the New York City Board of Education and the college, which is a unit of the City University of New York. The high school, housed physically within the college, serves 450 students recommended by two school districts adjacent to the college. The students have been identified as high-risk students, prone to dropout, yet with college potential. The school operates on a trimester model, similar to the college, and the core of the curriculum is career preparation, with one-third of the students out on internships at all times. Some of the students are eligible to take college courses, if counseled into them by the collaborative staff. If they choose to attend the college after high school completion, they are exempted from some college requirements and given advanced standing. The principal is jointly selected and participates in the college governance structure, and some of the faculty members at each level are shared. The college has also helped to develop an alternative high school designed to serve immigrant children with language skills problems.

North Carolina: Catawba Valley Technical College. Since North Carolina has attracted a large furniture industry, this college has developed programs to meet the needs of personnel and firms within the field. Courses are offered both at the college and in manufacturing plants in furniture drafting, product development, production management, upholstering, furniture design, and furniture marketing. The college laboratory is a small-scale factory in itself.

North Dakota: Bismarck State College. At Bismarck State College, a two-year public institution, two forty-five-week programs have been developed in power plant technology and process plant technology, with a fifteen-week core common to both. The former provides control-room operators for power-generating plants throughout the western part of the state, and the latter provides the same kinds of employees for the nation's first and only coal gasification plant at Beulah, North Dakota.

Pennsylvania: Williamsport Area Community College. This college has two noteworthy occupational-technical programs. Their plastics and polymer technology program, the only one in the state and one of only two on the East Coast, trains technicians to work with processing techniques such as injection molding, extrusion, vacuum forming, injection blow molding, and extrusion blow molding. The automated manufacturing technology program develops skills in quality control, computerized numerical control, robotic applications, computer-aided design, and computer-integrated manufacturing.

Rhode Island: Community College of Rhode Island. The J. Arthur Trudeau Memorial Center provides services for mentally retarded citizens. A new facility being constructed on college property will be used for nonresidential, vocational programs and job placement assistance for clients of the center. The center, which currently serves as a clinical site for student field placements, will be a "lab school" for students in the college's human services program. Expanded professional relationships between college faculty and center staff members have strengthened both.

Tennessee: Columbia State Community College. This college's Center of Emphasis develops and produces interdisciplinary, interactive video programs and computer-assisted productions through the collaborative efforts of the faculty in several departments and the center staff. Completed programs are then made available for student use in the center. The laboratory has twenty-four workstations with touch-screen monitors connected to computers and videocassette recorders (VCRs) for interactive experiences that supplement instruction on subjects as diverse as the anatomy of a cat and the battles of the Civil War.

Texas: Laredo Junior College. The college, with the support of the Texas Department of Agriculture, the Hebrew University in Israel, and Texas A&I at Kingsville, is developing and implementing a curriculum for teaching innovative agricultural approaches to students at the postsecondary level, utilizing a unique research and teaching facility—a 135-acre demonstration farm for small farmers and agricultural businesses located at the college. The farm emphasizes application of Israeli arid-land production technologies in comparable conditions in Texas. Laredo has noted that agricultural diversification in the state has the potential to create 25,000 new jobs, adding $6.1 billion of new business to Texas's economy by developing fourteen alternative crops in the arid regions of the Rio Grande Valley and West Texas. Discussions have already taken place with representatives of institutions of higher learning in Mexico to explore further dissemination of the results of this program.

Wisconsin: Milwaukee Area Technical College. The Milwaukee Enterprise Center was the brainchild of the Wisconsin State Board and the Wisconsin Foundation for Vocational, Technical, and Adult Education. The center acts as an incubator, providing low-cost space with a system of support services to new and emerging entrepreneurs and industries, especially to minority business, and to others offering employment opportunities to the handicapped and disadvantaged residents of the city. The facility was first occupied by five diverse businesses: a daycare–Head Start program, a food distributor, a knitting manufacturer, a wood products firm, and a recreational products firm, representing only one quarter of the available space. An Economic Development Administration grant, matched by money from the city of Milwaukee, helped to expand the representation to include other tenants, such as a robotics engineering firm, a plumbing-carpentry contractor, a medical distributor, and a group of artists.

Conclusion

Highlighting projects, programs, and services such as those described here ignores an equal number of good examples. One could have included the core curriculum at South Mountain Community College (Arizona), which focuses on effectively recruiting, retaining, and preparing students academically and socially while they are still in high school; the "Hawaii No Ka Oi" program at Kapiolani Community College, which offers informative workshops for those wanting to learn more about the islands' cultural heritage, multiethnic history, and natural environment; the program of individualized instruction at Bunker Hill Community College (Massachusetts), which includes over a thousand sequenced programs in a learning center staffed by professionals; Project Select at Westchester Community College (New York), which identifies potential teachers from among the community college student body, instructs them in a seminar jointly taught by faculty from a nearby university's school of education and a local school district, and then articulates with the education programs at the university, qualifying students for employment in the school district; the Wood Technology Program that trains operators of sawmills at Haywood Community College (North Carolina); and the National Training Center for Microelectronics at Northampton Community College (Pennsylvania), which offers training on a variety of levels, ranging from engineer through operator to technician, in surface mount technology, hybrid microelectronics, and semiconductor fabrication.

Still other innovative and unique programs are outlined in *Celebrating Two Decades of Innovation* (Goodwin, 1988), a publication listing some of the programs of member institutions of the League for Innovation in the Community College.

Taken together, these programs that make community colleges distinctive educational institutions are impressive. Some of them, such as the Process Plant Technology Program at Bismarck State College (North Dakota) or the Metrology Program at Butler County Community College (Pennsylvania), may be the only ones of their type in the nation. Others are clearly replicated, such as the Middle College High School at Shelby State Community College (Tennessee), which has acknowledged the leadership in the field given by LaGuardia Community College. Some institutions, such as the Danville Area Community College through the formation of its Area Labor-Management Council, serve as catalysts without doing everything themselves. Some states spread the scarce resources around, such as the Mobile Dental Hygiene Program in Kentucky. Others have institutions that cooperate with community agencies to achieve more than any one entity can do alone. For example, there is the Milwaukee area collaboration among the city, the community college, the Wisconsin Foundation for Vocational, Technical, and Adult Education, and area businesses; and the cooperative effort among Kellogg Community College, local school districts, and the public library. Some efforts are more than a dozen years old, while others are still in the process of formation.

All efforts, however, help to make their institutions true "community" colleges—distinct from other types of institutions and even from their brother and sister institutions. They also help fulfill the promise of the "open door." In so doing, they exemplify the work of the community colleges as described by Vaughan (1987): "Just as the Statue of Liberty beckoned those new to our shores, the community college beckons today.

> Give us your young, and your not so young;
> Give us your capable, and your not so capable;
> Give us your minorities, and your homemakers;
> Give us your employed, your underemployed,
>   your unemployed;
> Give us those in society who have too long lingered
>   on the periphery of the American Dream,
> And we will help them to become better students,
>   better workers, better citizens, better people."

References

American Association of University Professors. "The Annual Report on the Economic Status of the Profession: 1987-1988." *Academe*, 1988, 74 (2), 1-75.

Blocker, C. E., Plummer, R. H., and Richardson, R. C. *The Two-Year College: A Social Synthesis.* Englewood Cliffs, N.J.: Prentice-Hall, 1965.

Brick, M. *Forum and Focus for the Junior College Movement: The American Association of Junior Colleges.* New York: Teachers College Press, 1963.

Clark, B. R. *The Open-Door College: A Case Study.* New York: McGraw-Hill, 1960.

Cohen, A. M. "The Community College in the American Educational System." In G. T. Kurian (ed.), *Yearbook of American Universities and Colleges, Academic Year, 1986–87.* New York: Garland, 1988.

Fields, R. R. *The Community College Movement.* New York: McGraw-Hill, 1962.

Florida State Board of Community Colleges, Florida Association of Community Colleges, and Florida Department of Education. *Exemplary Programs of Florida's Community College System.* Tallahassee: Florida Department of Education, n.d.

Goodwin, G. (ed.). *Celebrating Two Decades of Innovation.* Laguna Hills, Calif.: League for Innovation in the Community College, 1988.

Maryland State Board for Community Colleges. "Maryland Community College Innovations Cited: The Honor Roll of Outstanding Achievements—Part I." *Maryland State Board for Community Colleges Bulletin,* February 1987a, p. 4.

Maryland State Board for Community Colleges. "Maryland Community College Innovations Cited: The Honor Roll of Outstanding Achievements—Part II." *Maryland State Board for Community Colleges Bulletin,* April, 1987b, p. 4.

Roueche, J. E., and Baker, G., III. *Access and Excellence: The Open-Door College.* Washington, D.C.: American Association of Community and Junior Colleges, 1987.

Stern, J. D., and Chandler, M. O. (eds.). *The Condition of Education: A Statistical Report.* Washington, D.C.: Center for Statistics (OERI/ED), 1987. 252 pp. (ED 284 371)

Vaughan, G. B. *The Community College in America: A Short History.* (Rev. ed.) Washington, D.C.: American Association of Community and Junior Colleges, 1985.

Vaughan, G. B. "The Community College and the American Dream." Unpublished paper. Washington, D.C.: American Association of Community and Junior Colleges, 1987.

Warren, J. "The Changing Characteristics of Community College Students." In W. L. Deegan, D. Tillery, and Associates (eds.), *Renewing the American Community College: Priorities and Strategies for Effective Leadership.* San Francisco: Jossey-Bass, 1985.

Joseph N. Hankin is president of Westchester Community College in Valhalla, New York.

Ascertaining both internal and external constituents'
perceptions of the institution may suggest new possibilities
for distinction.

A Search for Institutional Distinctiveness: Overview of Process and Possibilities

Barbara K. Townsend

Institutions, like people, change and develop over time. Often they begin as small organizations created through the efforts of a few dedicated individuals and then develop into complex organizations, employing thousands and serving diverse functions. Miami–Dade Community College started in 1960 on one campus serving 1,400 students. Now Miami–Dade is one of the ten largest colleges in the nation, with three campuses serving over 60,000 students (Miami–Dade Community College, 1987). Similarly, the institution of the public two-year college has developed from only a few colleges at the start of this century to over a thousand institutions serving over 4 million students in the late 1980s.

Much of the growth of the public two-year or community college occurred during the 1960s, a period when American belief in education as the means to a better life resulted in extensive funding of public higher education systems. During this period, community colleges were established at the rate of almost one a week. They emerged as educational

B. K. Townsend (ed.). *A Search for Institutional Distinctiveness.*
New Directions for Community Colleges, no. 65. San Francisco: Jossey-Bass, Spring 1989.

institutions determined to provide "something for everybody," including people not normally expected to attend college.

Their willingness to serve nontraditional students and to reach out into the community to recruit them was novel in the late sixties and much of the seventies. In the 1980s, however, it is a rare higher education institution that does *not* extend itself in numerous ways to these students. Thus, what once distinguished the community college as a type of educational institution no longer does. Indeed, currently about the only distinctive characteristics of the community college as an institutional type are the length of its academic programs (two years or less as compared to the four-year programs of a college or university), its low cost, and its diversity of curricular offerings.

Distinctiveness in program length is inherent in the conception of the community college: It was designed as a *two*-year school. It was also initially conceived of as a free or low-cost institution, which it still is today. Nationally, tuition costs at public two-year colleges averaged $660 in 1985–86 as compared to almost twice that amount at public four-year colleges and universities and almost eight times that amount at private four-year colleges and universities (American Association of Community and Junior Colleges, 1987). Finally, the community college's curricular offerings are the most diverse in postsecondary education. Its credit offerings include academic or transfer-level programs as well as a wide spectrum of occupational-technical programs. In addition, it offers developmental courses, adult basic education, and noncredit, leisure-time courses such as flower arranging and poetry writing.

While advocates of the community college may argue that it is also distinguished by its geographic and academic accessibility as well as by its community service orientation, in reality there are many four-year colleges and universities, both public and private, that are basically open-door institutions, accessible to and serving the needs of residents in their local community. In particular, many small, private, liberal arts colleges pride themselves on paying individual attention to students and being responsive to the needs of their surrounding community.

When the community college was highly distinctive as a type of educational institution, individual community colleges benefited from this generic distinctiveness through soaring enrollments and state funding. Now that the community college is less distinctive as an educational institution, individual community colleges are finding it more difficult to attract community members' enrollment in them as opposed to the local proprietary school or state college. The competition for state dollars has also increased as legislators and governors question why there should be so many state institutions of higher education performing essentially the same functions.

As a result, individual community colleges are ripe to search for institutional distinctiveness. It is time for them to break away from what was once a national institutional effort to provide "something for everybody" and move instead toward emphasizing, as individual institutions, those distinctive elements and qualities that they possess and that are valued by their local communities. Determining what distinctive elements and qualities a particular community college has and concentrating institutional resources to develop these and other distinctive aspects are important steps in the college's development.

Achieving institutional distinctiveness involves two major stages: first, conducting a search for distinctive elements and qualities—that is, determining whether the institution has some distinctive aspects, and, if so, what and how strong these aspects are—and, second, utilizing the information derived from this determination.

Conducting the Search for Distinctive Aspects

Deciding to conduct a search for institutional distinctiveness is the first step in determining what, if anything, is distinctive about a particular community college. Once that decision has been made, pragmatic logistical questions arise. Who should do the study? When should it occur? How long will it take? How should its results be disseminated? More substantively, the questions of focus and methodology arise: What information is being sought? How will it be elicited? While these questions will be addressed in detail in Chapters Four through Six, the following is a brief overview of the process suggested here.

Focus. Determining the existence, nature, and strength of an institution's distinctive aspects requires an understanding of what is meant by institutional distinctiveness and what conditions affect an institution's ability to be distinctive.

A distinctive institution is one that has distinguished itself from other institutions carrying out similar functions. It does so either by actually differing or by being perceived as differing on some of the elements or dimensions necessary for these institutions to carry out their common functions. While an educational institution can be distinctive for negative reasons, such as its illiterate graduates or its arrogant faculty, an underlying assumption of this book is that those leaders searching for institutional distinctiveness desire their institution to be viewed as differing positively from similar institutions on a particular element or dimension. The ideal is an institution perceived as offering something of value that other institutions in the local area or service region do not. For example, all higher education institutions offer academic programs. For a community college to be distinctive on this element, it must offer programs that other institutions in its area or region do not, or it must offer programs that differ (or are perceived to differ) substantively in their organizing framework, emphases, or structure from other institutions' programs with the same name. Similarly, all educational institutions have faculty teaching students. For a community college to be distinctive on this common element, there must be a tangible or perceived difference in the quality or nature of the faculty-student interaction.

It is important to understand that institutional distinctiveness has two dimensions: empirical and perceptual. Empirically an institution is distinctive if the elements or dimensions for which it claims distinctiveness have a basis in fact—that is, there is tangible "proof" of their existence. Obviously, a community college is distinctive empirically in its program offerings if it is the only postsecondary institution in its area, service region, or state to offer particular programs. It may also have an empirical distinctiveness if it is one of only a few institutions to offer services to a certain clientele.

An institution may also be *perceived* to be distinctive even when there is little or no empirical reality to this perception. For example, many community college faculty and administrators perceive their institution to offer students more individual attention and support than they would receive elsewhere in higher education. Not only are there few, if any, studies that support such claims, but faculty in small, private, liberal arts colleges also make the same claim. Thus, perceptions of institutional distinctiveness may not always match the reality.

Perceptions of an institution are important, though, because they can influence the empirical reality. If people believe that a certain situation exists at an institution, that situation may come into being. For example, if faculty and staff believe that a concern for students is a value of the institution's administration and will be recognized in annual evaluations, then at least some faculty and staff will increase their demonstrations of caring about students' academic success. The students will experience this increased caring and will then perceive the institution to be a caring one, which indeed it has also become in reality, although no studies may be conducted to "prove" that it is so.

In their search for institutional distinctiveness, institutional leaders need to ascertain which of their community college programs and other elements are empirically distinctive. Leaders also need to determine what elements and dimensions of the institution are perceived as being distinctive; in other words, they need to discover which institutional aspects have a distinctive image. The usual approach to examining institutional image is to determine the perceptions of external constituents—local citizens and leaders of business and industry—through image studies conducted by the office of institutional research. These perceptions can provide important information to institutional leaders, but they may not be congruent with the perceptions of internal constituents. Internal constituents—trustees, administrators, faculty, support staff, and students—

also need to be queried about their perceptions of the institution's distinctiveness. Their responses will yield a picture of the institution as perceived by those who have firsthand knowledge of its inner workings. While some of the constituents' perceptions may surprise and even dismay a college's leadership, which may hold a different vision of the institution, it is important for institutional leaders to understand how those within the institution perceive it.

These perceptions of internal constituents then need to be checked against the perceptions of external constituents. Those who are outside the institution may perceive elements as distinctive that those who are within may take for granted because they are too close to them. In addition, those outside may not value to the same degree an element or facet that those within the institution do. Ultimately, the goal of the search for institutional distinctiveness is to align the external and internal views of the institution's positive elements as closely as possible. Only in this way can an institution be sure it is giving the marketplace what it wants while also satisfying the preferences of its internal constituents.

Determination of external perceptions also reinforces the importance of the external environment to the development of institutional distinctiveness in the community college. While many four-year colleges and universities have state or national student bodies, most community colleges are local institutions, drawing their enrollments almost entirely from residents in their immediate community. As a result, the socioeconomic level of the community in which it is situated and the quantity and diversity of businesses and industries within this community have a strong impact on what the community college can become, both in terms of its programmatic offerings and others' perceptions of its distinctiveness as an educational institution. If a community college is located in an area with mostly blue- and pink-collar workers, these people will be likely students for the institution because they will value what it has to offer them. Its flexible scheduling will enable them to take courses while still working full time, its low cost will suit their pocketbooks, and its open-admissions policy will accommodate their previous academic record.

In addition, if the community has many varied businesses and industries that need training programs for their workers, the community college can become the higher education institution that offers these programs. A community college located in this kind of environment can easily achieve a distinctive image as an institution that meets the needs of local residents for inexpensive, easily accessible job training and college courses. On the other hand, a community college located in an area with few businesses and industries needing trained workers and with a low-cost, open-admissions state college nearby will find achieving a distinctive image in its community to be more difficult. Moreover, the degree of funding available from the state and from the locality may affect a community college's programmatic possibilities. Thus, the external environment—that is, where the community college is located—sets major parameters on the degree and type of institutional distinctiveness possible.

In some instances, the restrictions caused by the institution's geographic and socioeconomic setting may not allow for much distinctiveness in programmatic offerings. Distinctiveness can still be achieved, however, by differing qualitatively on important dimensions of the educational process. For example, constituents within a particular community college can agree to provide a highly supportive environment for first-generation college students of any ethnic background or age. If the community college is located in an ethnically diverse, working-class community, this supportive environment will be valued by community members and will become the college's distinctive element, even if the institution is not able financially to be distinctive by offering a wide variety of occupational-technical programs.

Methodology. Determining a community college's potential for achieving institutional distinctiveness involves three components: (1) searching for empirically distinctive programs, (2) ascertaining the perceptions of internal constituents about the institution, and (3) checking the perceptions of internal constituents against those of external constituents. While the perceptions of an institution's external constituents and those of its internal constituents are equally important, the methodology detailed in this book concentrates on the gathering of internal perceptions, a neglected topic in the community college's efforts to achieve a distinctive identity. Determination of external perceptions is then advocated as a kind of "reality check" of internal constituents' perceptions.

The easiest part of the search for institutional distinctiveness is looking for evidence of empirically distinctive programs and services. For example, Illinois community colleges are required to keep a list of "distinctive" programs on file with the Illinois Community College Board. The programs on the list are those in which out-of-district students may enroll at the "charge-back" price since the community college within their district does not have such programs. Seeking out this list is a logical step in an Illinois community college's search for empirically distinctive programs. Another way to ascertain such programs is to ask an institution's division heads and deans to generate a list of the distinctive programs in their area. These lists can then be verified by checking other area postsecondary institutions to see if they have similar programs.

Far more time consuming is ascertaining the perceptions of internal constituents about possible distinctive institutional elements and dimensions. Trustees, administrators, middle managers, classified staff, faculty, and students must be surveyed and interviewed for their perceptions regarding the institution's distinctive elements. The data derived from the interviews and surveys are then analyzed for themes and presented to at least some of the constituent groups such as the faculty and administrators for further refinement.

Institutional leaders must then assess the validity of internal constituents' perceptions of distinctive elements. For example, faculty may perceive they are distinctive in their frequent use of alternative modes of learning. Before deciding to promote the institution externally as distinctive because of the diverse ways it enables students to learn, administrators should first ask if there is any evidence to indicate that their institution's faculty do indeed use alternative modes of learning more frequently than do faculty at other postsecondary institutions. If there is little or no empirical evidence, then administrators concerned with institutional integrity have two choices. They can attempt to turn the faculty's perceptions into reality through rewarding faculty who do use alternative modes of learning, or they can refuse to claim distinctiveness for this aspect.

The third component of the process—checking internal perceptions of the institution against those of external constituents—provides another way of ascertaining the validity of internal perceptions. For example, if faculty and staff perceive themselves to offer a supportive environment for returning women, this perception can be checked as part of a survey of local residents, along with other questions about the college.

In sum, this first stage of the search for institutional distinctiveness will yield two kinds of information: what programs and elements, if any, are empircally distinctive, in a particular community college, and what elements and dimensions are perceived to be distinctive, both by internal and external constituencies.

Utilizing What the First Stage of the Search Reveals

In the second stage of the search for institutional distinctiveness, senior-level administrators utilize the information gained thus far. The search may reveal that the community college has several distinctive programs and other elements that are already receiving sufficient attention and recognition, both within the college and outside it. For example, institutional leaders may learn that their institution has several empirically distinctive programs and is also perceived by its faculty, staff, and students and by the local community to be a college that "goes the extra mile" for its students.

Institutional leaders who find themselves in the enviable position of already having distinctive programs and other elements have some decisions to make. First of all, they need to evaluate these distinctive programs and elements. A particular technical program may clearly be distinctive—that is, the only one in the college's service area—but it may generate insufficient enrollment to justify its high costs for equipment and staffing. Thus, senior-level administrators may decide to terminate the program in spite of its distinctiveness.

Another decision to be made is which distinctive elements should be emphasized in the marketing of the institution as well as in its internal workings. If faculty and staff perceive that they are distinctive in their caring attitude toward students, administrators may decide to emphasize this attitude by rewarding it in annual personnel evaluations. This same element could also be emphasized to external constituents in promotional literature about the college: Quotations from students about the caring faculty and staff could be included in college brochures and advertisements.

While some institutions that undergo a search for institutional distinctiveness will find their distinctiveness verified, the majority of institutions will probably be revealed as lacking much or any distinctiveness as educational institutions. They will lack empirically distinctive programs, and the elements perceived by their internal constituents as distinctive will have little basis in reality or will not be so perceived by the local community. If such is the case, institutional leaders have several options. One is to create and develop some empirically distinctive programs. For example, a needs assessment of local businesses and industries might indicate a demand for workers trained in robotics. After ascertaining that no other regional postsecondary institution provides such training, senior-level administrators may decide to pursue state funding for a program in robotics. Another approach is to decide to emphasize, both internally and externally, the elements perceived by internal constituents as distinctive. As suggested before, if faculty and staff perceive themselves to be more caring about the academic success of students than are faculty and staff in four-year colleges and universities, institutional leaders can elect to emphasize this dimension in the reward system. By so doing, administrators will be encouraging an empirical reality as well as a perceptual one. In addition, the institution's emphasis on providing a caring environment for the student can be stressed in its marketing of the institution.

In deciding to develop distinctive programs such as robotics and/or to emphasize less tangible elements such as a caring attitude toward students, senior-level administrators need to be aware of the different requirements for each. Developing empirically distinctive programs involves obvious, straightforward steps: Identify a community need, plan a program to meet this need, find funding for the program, and market it. Finding the funding is probably the major task and may be a Herculean one nowadays in some communities and states. However, if institutional leaders can find the money to establish empirically distinctive programs, whether they be academic ones or support services, institutional distinctiveness of a certain type is within their grasp.

Establishing institutional distinctiveness through emphasizing a qualitatively better dimension of such a standard function or element as teaching is a far more complex process. Administrators who decide to pursue this option must keep several points in mind. First, they should only emphasize an element that has the support of the majority of the institution's internal constituents. Deciding to emphasize in the local community a research orientation in the faculty would be unwise if most of the faculty are not committed to pursuing research.

Equally important is external or community demand for the element. Institutional leaders should guard against emphasizing a quality or dimension desired by internal constituents but not by the community. For example, those in charge of the curriculum may be enamored of self-paced learning. They may advocate that every course be self-paced—that is, with students working individually at their own pace with little or no interaction with other students in the classroom. Would-be students, however, may be wary of this approach to learning. Accustomed to the usual classroom interaction, they may regard with suspicion an institution that uses a less mainstream approach. Those who want to attend college partly for the opportunity it provides to make friends would also be alienated by self-paced learning, since it provides little opportunity for students to work with one another. Thus, an institution that uses only this approach to learning would certainly be a distinctive institution, but it puts its survival at risk if external constituents do not desire this approach. Educational leaders should remember the automobile industry's experience with the Edsel, a car touted by its makers as the latest in automotive design and sure to sell to the American public. Unfortunately for Ford, its maker, the Edsel's kind of distinctiveness did not appeal to car buyers. The car flopped on the market and quickly became an automotive dinosaur. The fate of the Edsel serves as a warning to institutional leaders seeking distinctiveness: Be sure that external constituents desire the distinctive element as much as internal constituents do.

Another consideration exists for institutional leaders seeking institutional distinctiveness: Careful long-range planning must ensure that there are sufficient institutional funds to maintain a distinctive element or dimension once it is developed. For example, leaders of an urban community college may decide to stress the institution's ability to provide support services for minority students. Initially, funds will be needed to create or expand support services for minorities. Spanish-speaking advisers and counselors might be hired, and computer programs that teach basic math in Spanish might be bought. Once these and other special services are in place, money must also be spent to ensure their continuance.

Finally, for those leaders concerned with institutional integrity, the perceptions (both internal and external) of an intangible element such as caring faculty and staff should match the reality. This requires ongoing evaluation as well as the willingness and the funds to support, through the reward system, faculty and staff who manifest the distinctive elements.

Conclusion

Since the community college is no longer as distinctive an educational institution as it once was, leaders at individual community colleges are urged to conduct a search for institutional distinctiveness. In so doing, they will learn what programmatic elements and dimensions are empirically distinctive or even unique about their institutions. They will also learn what dimensions are perceived by internal and external constituents to be distinctive, even though these dimensions may not be so in reality.

The decision to search for institutional distinctiveness involves the risk of learning what little, if anything, is empirically distinctive about a particular institution or that constituents' perceptions are inconsistent with the institutional vision held by its leaders. But the decision also opens up new possibilities for an institution. As its leaders decide to establish or build on perceived and empirically distinctive elements, they can develop an institution whose identity is a matter of personal and professional pride for all its members. Institutional leaders can also create an institution worthy of the positive public image so vital to institutional survival and development.

References

American Association of Community and Junior Colleges. *Community, Technical, and Junior College Fact Book*. Washington, D.C.: American Association of Community and Junior Colleges, 1987.

Miami-Dade Community College. *Miami-Dade Community College 1987–1988 Catalogue*. Miami, Fla.: Miami-Dade Community College, 1987.

Barbara K. Townsend is assistant professor of higher education at Loyola University of Chicago and is a former community college faculty member and administrator.

The initial organization for a community college's search for distinctiveness includes use of a college committee or a consultant.

How to Begin the Search for Institutional Distinctiveness

Michael B. Quanty

A college's search for institutional distinctiveness begins in earnest with the decision of how to proceed with the study. Although there are many possible ways to conduct such a search, the decision will probably be between appointing a college committee to explore the issue or employing a consultant from outside the college. Both approaches have advantages and disadvantages.

The appointment of committees to deal with complex issues is a time-worn tradition in education—almost to the point of being a cliché. Nevertheless, the practice has merit. Committee members will be more familiar with the college than will a consultant. Also, a committee can bring a wide range of perspectives and expertise to bear on a problem. Involving members of the college community in the search also could help build consensus on the findings and a sense of commitment to the project. On the other hand, the process of developing consensus often results in compromises on important issues. Committee members also may be so involved with the college that their objectivity is impaired. In addition, although they may be very familiar with their own college, they may have a limited perspective on what other colleges are doing. Since a

B. K. Townsend (ed.). *A Search for Institutional Distinctiveness.*
New Directions for Community Colleges, no. 65. San Francisco: Jossey-Bass, Spring 1989.

definition of distinctiveness requires differentiating one's college from other institutions, this limited perspective can be a serious problem.

An outside consultant can bring specialized expertise and a fresh, objective perspective to the search. A consultant also is more likely to be sufficiently familiar with other institutions to identify clearly distinctive characteristics of the college. The level of accountability for the consultant who is employed specifically for the task is also likely to be higher than that of a committee composed of individuals with many other responsibilities. On the negative side, the college community may react to a consultant with skepticism, especially if her or his findings turn out to be at variance with the conventional wisdom on campus. People who have invested a great deal of themselves in an institution may question the assumption that someone from the outside can, with limited exposure, develop a better understanding of the college than they possess.

A key consideration in the choice between these two approaches is the college's past experience with committees and consultants. These experiences obviously will affect the college's receptivity to one or the other process. The prevailing mood of the campus is another important consideration. If the college is relatively mature in its development, fiscally sound, with healthy enrollments and good job security, having an outside consultant lead the search may be perceived as a good idea. If the environment is unstable, employing a consultant could be seen as threatening. If the situation at the college is desperate, a consultant may be seen as the only viable option. Under any circumstances, the decision as to who will conduct the search is a crucial one and should be weighed carefully.

Using a College Committee

If the decision is made to use a college committee to conduct the search for distinctiveness, each of the following areas must be addressed if the committee's work is to have maximum impact: (1) selecting its members, (2) developing the committee's charge, (3) organizing the committee effectively, (4) providing the committee with the necessary background information, (5) providing the necessary institutional support, and (6) developing a procedure for achieving consensus on the committee's findings.

Selecting the Committee. The first decision in choosing a committee involves representation. Criteria for selection should be carefully considered and clearly stated. Often committees are structured so that members collectively represent a variety of perspectives and are balanced according to such factors as race, sex, type of discipline, and division. Nevertheless, individual committee members may never know whom they are supposed to represent. Is a black male faculty member who teaches English representing blacks, teaching faculty, the English Department, or some other group? In fact, given the selection process, he or she most likely will be perceived as representing several perspectives at once. During committee deliberations, he may also represent each of his perceived constituencies at different points. Such amorphous role expectations obviously can create confusion. To avoid such confusion, the college administration should fully apprise committee members of the reasons for their selection.

The nature of a committee's assignment should determine the composition of the committee and the criteria for selecting its members. In this case, the committee will be asked to determine what about the college is distinctive and to communicate its findings to the college community. For the first task, one needs individuals who are analytical and who represent a wide spectrum of views. For the second task, one needs individuals who have credibility with various constituencies on campus and who are effective communicators.

To assure a wide spectrum of views and to facilitate later acceptance of the findings, the committee must include representatives of faculty, support staff, and administrators. Distinctive aspects of a college are probably not limited to its instructional programs, so the committee should not be limited only to faculty. Faculty membership should include a representative from each division and people from both occupational-technical and college transfer disciplines. Support staff should include at least one representative from each dean's or vice-president's area. Administrative membership should be limited to one or two individuals who have a broad understanding of the college.

The criteria for selecting individual members from all three groups are the same. As mentioned earlier, the task requires that they have good analytical abilities. The second criterion is that they should be opinion leaders, individuals who have a reputation for clearly articulating their views and for influencing opinion on important issues. These individuals should not be confused with the opinionated spokespeople who may consistently and vociferously represent a particular point of view but who seldom influence the outcomes of a vote. Opinion leaders also should not be confused with the elected or appointed leadership of recognized organizations such as a faculty or staff senate. Although opinion leaders often do assume these roles, not all elected leaders are effective opinion leaders. An opinion leader is one who is seen as thoughtful, insightful, and reasonable even by those who may differ with the person on an issue, one who is forceful but open to other points of view and able to compromise. Choosing these types of individuals ensures that various points of view will be well represented within the committee while minimizing the chances of factionalism disrupting the group.

It is obvious from the preceding discussion that my bias for committee selection for this purpose is by appointment rather than election. The skills required for this task are such that election does not seem appropriate. The president, however, should not attempt to appoint the members alone. A good approach would be to work with the college's deans or vice-presidents and the faculty and staff leaders to solicit nominations of people whom they feel possess the skills required, thus providing a pool of potential members. Individuals who are consistently nominated should prove good bets.

Another obvious point is that students were not included in the committee membership. This omission is not meant to minimize their importance in the process. It means that there are more effective and meaningful ways to include student participation than by having a few students serve on the committee. Committee membership would be a hardship for most community college students, and it would be difficult, if not impossible, to represent the full range of student views on a committee. Preferably, the committee should assume the responsibility for ensuring student involvement. They can do so in a variety of ways: surveys, interviews with selected students or student leaders, an open hearing for students, or a poll in the student newspaper, to name just a few. Ascertaining student opinion is too important to trust to the sporadic participation of one or two students on the committee.

Developing the Committee's Charge. The charge to the committee should be carefully stated in writing. It should clearly state why there is a need for the study, exactly what is expected of the committee, how the findings will be reviewed, and how they will be used.

Clearly articulating the need for such an undertaking will show the committee members and the college community that this is not a frivolous or hastily conceived idea. A carefully crafted statement of need can also allay concerns over hidden agendas and can stave off discussions about "why are we really doing this."

It is important to define carefully what is expected of the committee. The concept of distinctiveness is one that is not commonly associated with community colleges where emphasis traditionally has been placed on comprehensiveness. Therefore, great care should be taken to expand on the definition. It may also be useful to define the term by exception. Through an enumeration of many of the things that cannot be substituted for the institution's definition of its distinctive elements, the search can be better focused, and several false starts may be eliminated. For example, the following points might be made:

1. *Distinctiveness goes beyond mission.* The college's distinctiveness will not be found in its mission statement. The way a college operationalizes the various goals in its mission statement, the priorities it establishes among those goals, and the relative success it experiences in achieving different goals may contribute to its distinctiveness. The goals themselves, however, are not likely to set an institution apart.

2. *Distinctiveness goes beyond stereotypes.* Stereotypical statements such as "we offer excellent instruction because our faculty are paid to teach, not to do research" are not acceptable definitions for this purpose. The committee must be careful to avoid such generalizations.

3. *Distinctiveness is not a measure of work environment.* As the committee proceeds with its task, it is likely that members will discuss what is distinctive about the college to them. In these discussions or in subsequent interviews or discussions with one's colleagues, it is important to keep in mind that, while the work environment can permeate everything we do and how we are perceived, it usually is not a defining characteristic of a college. Only in cases where the work environment represents an attitude that also is reflected in programs and services does it become a defining characteristic.

4. *Distinctiveness is not a lightning bolt.* It is not likely that there will be a single program or service at the college that truly sets the institution apart. If a community college has such a program, chances are good that its members know about it. More likely, distinctiveness lies in having a unique grouping of programs or services, in an attitude about students or instruction that cuts across the college, or in the way the college orders its priorities.

This process of defining by exception may seem heavy-handed and smack of overkill, but it serves several purposes. It points out the need for careful research and consideration, it clarifies for the cynics that the search is not intended to be just another semantic exercise, and it helps the committee maintain the proper focus. The natural tendency would be to use such examples in an informal, oral presentation to the committee when the charge is explained. They really should be in writing, however, because inevitably, months into the task, committee members will be discussing what is really wanted. At that point, they won't accurately remember what was said and will look to what was written for guidance.

As part of defining the task, the charge to the committee should also explain the need for supporting evidence. It may be desirable to be less explicit in defining what will serve as evidence and merely stress the need for documentation. Through too narrow a definition of the type of evidence required, the scope of the study may inadvertently be circumscribed. For example, the committee may avoid qualitative judgments if too much emphasis is placed on quantifiable evidence.

The charge to the committee also should include a statement of how the findings will be reviewed. It may be desirable to include provisions for collegewide hearings on a draft of the report with a subsequent opportunity for the committee to reconsider and revise. The process for administrative review should be stated so that both the committee and the administrative staff know their respective roles. Finally, the president's responsibility for responding to the committee should be defined.

The final element of the charge should be a short statement of how the results will be used. This statement should include the intended audience for the report and the areas in which it will be used to influence decisions. This section is important because it could affect the way the committee approaches its task and because it will avoid future misunderstandings. The findings conceivably could be used in planning, budgeting and staffing, marketing, and fund raising and development. Similarly, the intended audience could be the president only or broad distribution within and outside the college. Knowing the range of uses in advance will probably affect the tone and nature of the report, but it will also make the committee more comfortable in its work.

Organizing the Committee. The way a committee is organized can have a substantial impact on the quality of the final report. Therefore, it is essential that the committee chair be able to conduct an effective meeting, to motivate people, and to delegate responsibilities. Just as in the case of selecting committee members, appointment rather than election is appropriate for this task. Since the process for accomplishing the task will be loosely defined, it places a great deal of responsibility on the chair. Not everyone can provide effective leadership in an unstructured situation. In fact, it might be a good idea to select the chair first and then to involve that person in the selection of other committee members.

In organizing a committee, one needs to remember the major advantages a committee offers. Those advantages include bringing a variety of perspectives to bear on a problem and creating a situation where brainstorming can develop individuals' ideas more fully. Too often committees are divided into small groups to work on a portion of the task and to bring a solution back to the group. The subcommittee reports are then spliced together to make a final report. The resulting product, then, is largely a collection of individuals' opinions about a variety of topics rather than a consensus of group opinion on the full range of topics. It is true that tasks need to be apportioned among the committee's members, but there needs to be a mechanism for assuring that the entire committee discusses and reviews the findings of any subgroups that are formed. The emphasis needs to be placed on this review and discussion rather than on merely completing a series of assigned tasks.

One way to help maintain the proper perspective is to have subcommittees prepare abbreviated reports that briefly state findings, evidence, and potential implications in a format similar to a sentence outline. This procedure will focus discussion on the findings, interpretations, and implications rather than the syntax, style, and tone of the report. The full committee can then arrive at consensus regarding major conclusions to be drawn from the subgroup's work. This system avoids having individuals and subgroups invest inordinate amounts of time in writing and places the emphasis where it should be: on review and synthesis.

Later a writing team or editor will be able to use the modified subgroup reports as outlines for developing a coherent report that reflects the views of the entire committee.

Providing the Committee with Background Information. The committee can save a great deal of time and increase its chances of success if its members are provided with an advance packet of background information, including an annotated bibliography of general articles and books on image and distinctiveness. Reprints of selected articles should also be provided. In addition, copies of selected institutional research studies conducted at the college should be included. Information relevant to internal perceptions can be found in student surveys, faculty and staff surveys, and graduate follow-ups. External perceptions can be documented in studies dealing with the success of graudates in the workplace and at transfer colleges, employer surveys, or image surveys conducted in the community. It might be helpful to have the institutional research office (or other office responsible for the surveys) prepare a short summary of findings related to internal and external perceptions and referencing specific reports. Relevant sections of the reports could be highlighted.

Another potentially valuable source of information for the group would be the college's self-study for accreditation or reaffirmation of accreditation. Sections reviewing the mission, educational programs, and support services could prove especially useful. The report of the visiting committee would provide an outside opinion and could point to areas that were deemed especially strong or distinctive.

Finally, the committee should be provided with relevant historical documents that would show changes in the college's emphasis or mission over time. Potential sources of such information would be long-range plans, curriculum plans, curriculum committee minutes, past mission statements, consultants' reports, and program reviews.

Providing the committee with this type of information not only makes its job easier but also reinforces the importance of its work and shows an institutional commitment to the project.

Providing Institutional Support to the Committee. For the committee to function effectively, it needs full institutional support. It is very likely that the committee will want to survey selected groups to help identify distinctive elements. The college should facilitate this effort by assigning the institutional research office (or other appropriate office) to provide staff support to the committee. If there is no office on campus that has the necessary expertise, the committee should have the option of employing a consultant.

The president also should ensure that other offices and the faculty and staff in general are prepared to cooperate with the committee. Urging of cooperation can be accomplished formally or informally, but it is critical that a spirit of cooperation prevails.

Achieving Consensus on the Report. For the report on distinctiveness to have maximum impact, the college needs to devise a method for achieving consensus on the findings. The process recommended here involves three elements: collegewide review, administrative review, and presidential reaction. Collegewide review can be accomplished through open hearings to review the findings. Such hearings would give the committee a chance to receive reactions of colleagues and provide an opportunity for it to reconsider its findings. Administrative review can be coordinated through the president and the chief administrative officers of the college. Once the president has the committee's final report and the reactions of the administrators, she or he should respond formally to the committee by stating reactions to the report and reasons for rejecting any recommendations. This reaction document then will serve as the college's position on its distinctiveness.

This review process is an essential element. It assures that the college community is aware of the college's position and brings closure to the process. It can help eliminate later confusion and debate and allow the college to begin the work of applying the insights gained from the search.

Using a Consultant

Perhaps the decision is made to employ a consultant rather than to use a committee. Choosing the right consultant and creating the climate for that individual or firm to perform its job require a great deal of effort on the part of the college. First, the college needs to determine the criteria that will be used to select the consultant. It then needs to develop a procedure for selecting among qualified candidates. Once a selection has been made, the college needs to provide necessary background information, establish the climate for the consultant's visit and subsequent report, arrange for a site visit, and evaluate the consultant's performance.

Determining Selection Criteria. The determination of selection criteria for the consultant will depend primarily on the purpose of the study and the intended use of the information. If the purpose is to determine what various constituencies *perceive* to be distinctive about the college and the information is to be used primarily in marketing the college, the consultant should be a marketing expert in developing corporate identities. If the purpose is to determine how the college *actually* differs from other educational institutions and the information is to be used primarily for institutional planning and budgeting activities, the consultant should be an educational expert.

In reality, of course, the college will probably wish to look at both perceptions and structural indications of distinctiveness and will want to use the information in a variety of ways. In such cases, the institution should establish tentative priorities among the intended purposes and uses of the study to serve as a guide for determining the needed qualifications of the consultant.

Qualifications that should be stressed regardless of the consultant's background are a familiarity with survey or interview methods, an ability to communicate with diverse constituencies, and good analytical skills. It is most important that the individual or group chosen have credibility within the college community. A good way to establish such credibility is to have a group at the college define the range of tasks required, the qualifications needed, and the procedure that will be used to make the selection.

Developing the Selection Procedure. A good method of selecting a consultant is to begin by developing a formal request for proposals. Developing a request will help the college clarify its expectations and will aid in determining the role and scope of responsibilities for the consultant. The first section of such a request should clearly spell out the study's objectives. Essentially, this section should describe what the consultant's final report to the college should cover. It should define what is meant by distinctiveness and provide an indication of how the information will be used.

The second section should request prospective consultants to propose a methodology for accomplishing the study objectives. If there are certain requirements that must be met, such as interviews with faculty, staff, or students, these should be stated. The request, however, should allow as much flexibility as possible in order to provide respondents with the opportunity to propose creative methodologies. The request should require respondents to define their role and the responsibilities of the college in the process. Respondents also should submit a tentative schedule for accomplishing the task within the time frame set by the college.

The third section should enumerate the criteria to be used in evaluating the proposals and the relative importance of each criterion. It should also state who will ultimately approve the report and determine that the conditions of the contract have been fulfilled.

Once a selection has been made, a formal contract should be prepared from the proposal. The consultant's search then can begin.

Providing Background Information for the Consultant. Before the consultant visits the campus for interviews, the college should provide her or him with enough information to ensure familiarity with the institution. The information packet should include a current college catalogue, promotional publications and brochures, annual reports, self-studies, program reviews, relevant research reports, and news articles or press releases. It might be advisable to request the consultant to prepare a brief initial-impressions report based on these materials.

Establishing the Climate for the Consultant's Visit. For the consultant's visit to be productive, the college community needs to be fully informed and receptive. Much of this work should have been accomplished during the development of the proposal. At the visitation stage, the president needs to reinforce the importance of the study and to establish the credibility of the process and the credentials of the consultant. The president should affirm that the consultant has full administrative support and urge full cooperation. Faculty and staff also should be assured that they will be given an opportunity to become involved and that individual responses to the consultant's questions will be kept confidential.

Arranging the Site Visit. The site visit should begin with a tour of the campus and end with a short debriefing in which the consultant gives an oral report summarizing general impressions of the visit. The activities in between, such as interviews with students, faculty, and administrators, will have been specified in the proposal and contract between the consultant and the college. Some provision should be made during the visit for allowing individuals to talk informally with the consultant. For example, the consultant could make time available for drop-in visits or provide a phone number for setting up appointments.

Evaluating the Consultant's Performance. The criteria for evaluation of the consultant's report will be specified in the contract. The committee or individual reviewing the report should hold strictly to these criteria. Any reservations should be submitted in writing and reviewed orally with the consultant before the final report is submitted. The college should require that the terms of the contract be met but should be careful not to increase its expectations at this point.

The consultant's report should not be viewed as the final product. The committee or individual to whom the consultant reports should use that report as the basis for a statement of the college's position. That statement may agree fully with the consultant's report or reject it completely. This latter statement, however, should be the focus of the college's subsequent discussions. From this point on, the reaction to the consultant's report would be the equivalent of a report developed entirely by a college committee and procedures to achieve consensus would be the same as those outlined previously.

Conclusion

A college's search for distinctiveness is a major undertaking. The procedures outlined in this chapter provide a framework for beginning the search and suggest methods for assuring appropriate involvement of key college constituencies in the search. Chapter Five will detail ways the committee or consultant can gather and analyze appropriate data in the institution's search for distinctiveness.

Michael B. Quanty is coordinator of institutional research and planning at Thomas Nelson Community College in Hampton, Virginia.

Information in a search for institutional distinctiveness can be garnered through institutional histories, needs assessments, institutional impact studies, marketing studies, and strategic planning studies.

Getting the Facts, Analyzing the Data, Building the Case for Institutional Distinctiveness

James L. Ratcliff

When Community College Philosophy Is Not Enough

Delbert Brunton lost his job over institutional distinctiveness. In the early 1900s Brunton was considered a pioneer in the junior college movement. As superintendent of Fullerton Union High School District in California, he not only founded Fullerton Junior College (FJC) but was also influential in the establishment of other early California junior colleges. Yet, in 1916, Brunton was relieved of his duties because he had advocated the merger of FJC with neighboring Santa Ana Junior College to form an Orange County junior college district. The proposal was perceived as a threat to FJC's identity and distinctiveness. In a hotly contested school board election, Fullerton voters defeated the proposal. Brunton was subsequently removed from office because he did not fully understand the Fullerton community attachment to its college (Plummer, 1949).

Understanding the specific, continuous value of a college to its community rather than merely the community's responsiveness to its pro-

B. K. Townsend (ed.). *A Search for Institutional Distinctiveness.*
New Directions for Community Colleges, no. 65. San Francisco: Jossey-Bass, Spring 1989.

grams and curricula is part of understanding the distinctive qualities that an institution such as FJC brings to the community it serves. Descriptive studies of community needs or satisfaction may mask divisiveness among community groups. In such situations, colleges and educational leaders cannot afford merely to respond according to educational philosophy, democratic platitudes, or concepts of how to proceed rationally. Brunton lost his job following such a course.

This chapter explores the all-important task of gathering valid information about the identity of a community college, verifying it, and building a case for the distinctive or even unique contributions of the college to its constituencies. Because different community groups hold different values of the college, formulating an overall vision of what makes the college distinctive is a significant information-gathering activity.

The Searcher's Mind-Set

We recognize the common and unique identity of a local community college when we form a concept of its history, development, and traditions. For most community colleges, identity either started in the 1960s and 1970s or in the 1920s and 1930s, the two major periods of growth in the number of colleges (Ratcliff, 1987a). For the colleges established in the 1920s and 1930s, the common vision of their distinctiveness is usually divided between their junior college period and their contemporary community college period. This very division implies progress, a development of the college and its curricula to meet an expanding range of constituencies. For the colleges created in the 1960s and 1970s, identity is often a contrast to other forms of higher education; access, opportunity, and "something for everyone" predominate. Thus, in the most elementary view, institutional identity is merely a collection of past facts about the college.

In reality, there are two sources of information on the college's past that add to our understanding of institutional identity. First, there is the college's institutional history, written or unwritten, which may be a dry chronicle of accolades to past leaders. If published, it was usually done so with funds from the college foundation and circulated among assorted alumni, civic leaders, and college officials to celebrate a particular anniversary of the college's birthdate. Now, a copy is in the college library, and another is on a bookshelf in the president's office. A second concept of institutional identity is derived from speeches. The college president, together with the chief executive officer of a local corporation, may proclaim a new business-industry partnership to be "historic." Here, the leaders are making an active attempt to impress the identity of the college, to advance it, to mark the transition of the college to a new level of service to a constituent.

There is a temptation to take this information at face value, but saying that the college is unique in this or that way does not make it so. Identity comes out of the context in which the college exists, and gathering data to make a case for institutional identity must go beyond the collection of accolades or the pronouncements from speeches whose intentions are legitimately promotional. The sense of a college's identity must be derived from more than the past statements of its import by its leaders or the chronicle of past college events by its antiquarian. Institutional introspection alone will not suffice as the basis for institutional identity. As Sir Herbert Read (1948) suggested in his utopian novel, *The Green Child*, "We roll our eyes inward until we become blind."

What does this caution mean for data gathering? First, it suggests that we need sources outside the institution. What have the local newspapers said about the college over the years? What have local representatives to the legislature said? How are they the same or different? Second, we must have more than one piece of evidence to corroborate our statements. Do the newspaper editors, the presidents of chambers of commerce, and the local high school principals agree on what the role and identity of the college is? Third, we must place college events within the context of the larger society. For example, it is not a coincidence that the focus of community colleges in the 1960s and 1970s was on educational opportunity and access; these were the nation's priorities as the civil rights movement and the returning veterans of the Vietnam War predominated in the student population. So the first task in preparing for data gathering is to place the college within the major social, political, economic, and technological events of the times. This should be done in such a fashion as to answer three questions: What was happening in the nation at the time? What was happening in the state at the time? What was happening locally and within the college district at the time? Each of these questions needs to be answered from several sources of information, such as newspapers, history books and articles, and interviews with key decision makers.

Locating Source Material

Where does one find the facts about the distinctiveness or uniqueness of a particular community college? If the investigator is part of the college professional staff rather than an outside consultant, then he or she is an eyewitness. That role carries with it all the biases that accrue from being involved in the daily operation of the college, but it also allows the researcher to know the inner workings of the institution, its staff, and several segments of the communities it serves.

Being on the scene permits firsthand interviews with the current players in the day-to-day institutional drama that constitutes the organizational climate of the college. Again, firsthand reports provide perspectives and information not available in documents, but they also carry with them the limitations of the view of the moment and the biases of those interviewed.

The shortest path to the facts that leads beyond the limitations of eyewitness narratives and interviews with citizens and college officials is library research. Such research may consist of econometric data collected by the local financial institution. It may also consist of the articles on the college found in the morgue of the local newspapers. Area newspapers covering earlier periods of the college can be located in *Newspapers on Microform* (Library of Congress, 1976) and may be obtained through interlibrary loans from state archives, universities or the state historical society. Such research may also involve data gathered from institutional histories and from needs assessments, institutional impact studies, marketing research, or strategic planning studies. Each of these activities is discussed later. But first there are some basic considerations in making efficient use of time in collecting the facts.

Since one cannot step up to the card catalogue in the college library and find a book entitled *What Makes this College Unique*, some sleuthing is required. Think about the major functions of the college: transfer, career programs, adult education, developmental education, career guidance, and so forth. Ask what makes the college unique for each function. What sources of information would reveal what makes the college unique in its transfer programs? Follow-up studies, conducted over the years, may contain anecdotal information from former students. Correspondence between the arts and sciences dean and neighboring four-year colleges and universities may unearth comments regarding the merits of college programs, faculty, or students. Letters from former students to individual faculty members or to the student newspaper may also provide direct evidence of the college's uniqueness in learning environment. Such information may be missed in a survey of students or in student exit interviews because the questions used on such instruments may overlook some aspects of the college that students find unique.

To gather a number of "snapshots" of the college over time, conduct an Educational Resources Information Center (ERIC) search using the college name (and its former names) as both institutional descriptors and as subject titles. For those colleges first established in the 1920s, 1930s, and 1940s, Walter Crosby Eells (1930) constructed a bibliography on junior colleges that is indexed by college and city; this bibliography was updated in the *Junior College Journal* from 1930 to 1945. Look also at studies by the state agency responsible for administering community college education to pick up any possible comparative information about different colleges within the state system. If one is researching a public community college, there will be facts about the college in the annual reports of the state legislative committees on education, the annual state blue book, and the annual reports of the state agency responsible for community college education.

Organizing the Data

Whether institutional distinctiveness is described and sought through a self-study, an institutional history, a needs assessment, a marketing plan, or a strategic planning document, one thing remains: The report on the search often becomes the sole source on the subject of the college's identity. The temptation is to allow the college to appear in its most positive light, to portray it as universally influential on the constituencies it serves. Yet the task of assembling the evidence of institutional distinctiveness is and should be one of ferreting out the truth from the evidence. Since the end result may be the sole source of information on college identity, it must be convincing, compelling, and accurate.

Few stop to reflect on how many times decisions have been based on a single technical report or planning document. Only the author of the report is scrutinized, and the power of the written word seduces those who wish to believe that, because it is published, it must be accurate. As Barbara Townsend stated in Chapter Three, many colleges may undergo a search for institutional distinctiveness only to find little confirmation of the uniqueness of their programs and services. Such an untoward finding, if glossed over in a report, may further weaken the college by failing to exhort it to design, address, and assert the value of its contributions.

As seasoned educators, we have learned to read with doubt editorials and political statements about the value of the local community college to the educational enterprise of the area. This healthy skepticism should carry over to our own writing, planning, and analysis.

Recently, a state legislator argued that Northeast Iowa Technical Institute (NITI), which was seeking to change its mission to that of a comprehensive community college, should be disbanded and the district should be divided among two other community college districts. His rationale was that, as a technical institute, the institution was distinct from the six private liberal arts colleges of the area, but, as a comprehensive community college, the institution would compete unnecessarily for students with the private colleges. What kind of evidence or data was there to support or reject the legislator's statement? One possible interpretation of the case was that NITI, once transformed into a community college, *would* compete with the private colleges because of its lower cost and wider range of programs. Another possible interpretation was that NITI really wouldn't be competing: The students who had attended it as a technical institute would be the same ones who would attend it as a community college. These current students would be joined by individuals who otherwise would not be able to attend college at all. Either argument requires more data, and be assured that the legislator who sought to block NITI's change of mission required convincing evidence that the mission change would not harm the operation of the private institutions!

If sometime in the future an institutional history were prepared for NITI, the author of that history would no doubt encounter the statements of the legislator in the local newspapers. Indeed, this legislator's position continues to have a great deal of influence on the destiny of NITI and the Iowa community college system. The historian can do one of several things with the legislator's statement: (1) Accept it as truth because it appeared in the local newspaper, (2) reject it because it did not correspond with what the author thinks is the college's distinctiveness, (3) suspend judgment about the validity of the legislator's accusations until further evidence corroborates the statement, or (4) ignore the statement because the historian judges the legislator's opposition to the mission change not to be important. The options relative to this piece of information illustrate the importance of suspending judgment about the value of evidence until corroborating and independent information confirms its validity. The researcher who seeks to establish institutional distinctiveness must reach a decision about the value and role of each piece of information; the amassed evidence must be convincing not only to college leaders but also to a wide range of constituencies, including opponents and competitors of the college.

Using Information-Gathering Activities

A variety of activities can provide the needed information in an institution's search for distinctiveness. This section looks at the use of institutional histories, needs assessments, institutional impact studies, marketing studies, and strategic planning studies.

Institutional Histories. Institutional histories can provide a rich background for uncovering and portraying institutional distinctiveness. A faculty member teaching state history and government may have the disciplinary background and skills to conduct an effective institutional history. The person needs to know what was happening in the state and in the community during the various periods of the college's existence.

Secondary sources of information can help place the college within the context of local, state, and national events. If the college began in the early period (1920s and 1930s), then a social history covering the period from its inception to at least the historian's memory of significant national events will be helpful. Richard Hofstader's *Age of Reform* (1955) or Eric Goldman's *Rendezvous with Destiny* (1956) are good examples of such social histories.

Next, seek out a good social history of the state in which the college is located. Look for studies of education in the state in order to place the college's identity within the context of other educational institutions. Dissertations are often a good source of this information and can be readily identified through a computer search of *Dissertation Abstracts International* (DAI). In DAI will be studies of whole states, such as A. E. Reid's (1966) "A History of the California Public Junior College Movement," or of single institutions, such as E. C. Strobel, Jr.'s (1975) "Wayne County Community College: A History of Its Antecedents, Establishment, and Early Development in the Metropolitan Detroit Setting." A particularly good source of information is the profiles of colleges and special college programs that have appeared in the *Community, Technical, and Junior College Journal* over the years. Also, the college and the state agency that governs the college system may have filed reports contained in the ERIC Clearinghouse system.

Primary data gathering can start with board minutes. By reading board minutes, one can get a notion of what were critical incidents or decisions that seemed to set the course of the institution. Not only critical incidents but also recurring themes and trends are important to note.

Once critical incidents and recurring issues have been identified, they can then be investigated through a variety of sources. First are the local newspapers. If the college district incorporates more than one town or if there is more than one newspaper, multiple views on key events can be collected through stories about the college appearing in the paper, letters to the editor by citizens and officials, and editorials about the college. Such activities also make good field learning experiences for students in college history or political science classes.

Needs Assessments. Needs assessments are periodically conducted by a college to determine the demand for various programs and services. Most frequently, needs assessments are used in planning continuing education, establishing the need for new career programs, or documenting service to specific community clientele. A needs assessment can provide an ideal opportunity to analyze and describe institutional distinctiveness as well.

Typically, needs assessments are surveys of one or most community groups served by the college, such as current students, graduating high school students, small-business owners, major area employers, and labor and professional organizations. In a needs assessment, it is particularly important to gather information about people's behavior as well as their interests. Asking adults which courses, programs, or services they would like the college to provide will undoubtedly result in a long list of "needs." But a question asking the same adults to describe what learning activities they have engaged in over the past twelve months will provide a more accurate gauge of the respondents' behavior. Querying area residents about their learning preferences and about their learning practices are separate questions; one deals with the future and good intentions, while the other examines past behavior. Although both are important, questions regarding behavior are generally more reliable.

To disclose institutional distinctiveness, one must differentiate between the community college and other forms of higher education. Validation comes through the cross-tabulation of data from multiple sources. NITI sought to change its mission to that of a community college. In determining the need for such a change, graduating high school seniors were asked if they planned to attend college on graduation and which of twenty-five colleges in a 150-mile radius they planned to attend (Ratcliff, 1987b). This data showed what proportion of students were planning to attend community colleges, technical institutes, four-year liberal arts colleges, and public universities. These students were also given a list of one- and two-year vocational programs, associate of applied science degree programs, and career programs that allowed students to transfer to a baccalaureate program. The students were also asked to give their grade-point average (GPA) in high school and the high school curriculum in which they were enrolled. Students planning to attend community colleges and technical institutes of the area were compared according to reported GPA, high school curriculum, probability of attending college, college of second choice, and degree program preference. No significant difference was found between high school students planning to go to community college and those planning to go to the technical institutes. Three out of four students, however, preferred attending a community college over attending the technical institute. Significant differences were found in GPA, high school curriculum, probability of attending college, college of second choice, and degree program preference among those planning to attend NITI and those planning to attend either the private four-year liberal arts colleges or the public universities. Institutional differentiation between two-year and baccalaureate-granting institutions had been determined. The students also clearly preferred the contemplated mission change.

The data gathered from high school students constituted only one constituency served by NITI. To verify and validate the findings of the high school survey, the needs assessment asked comparable questions of current students at NITI to determine if their past behavior matched the high school students' current preferences. The results regarding high school GPA, curriculum, college preference, postsecondary program interests, and probability of attending college were confirmed in the survey of current students. Skepticism, however, must reign in data gathering. One could argue that the majority of current students were separated from the high school seniors by a mere one to five years of age difference, since the majority of current NITI students surveyed were recent high school graduates. For this reason, comparable questions were again posed to the

NITI alumni. Here again, many of the same programs emerged as areas of interest, the same profile of student choice about college attendance was exhibited, and comparable high school curriculum, GPA, and probability of attending college were exhibited.

By using three or more data sources, by asking questions regarding college preference and program preference, and by cross-tabulating the data (rather than reporting simple percents of response), a needs assessment can provide valid and valuable information regarding the uniqueness of the college and its programs.

Institutional Impact Studies. An institutional impact study can also shed much light on the distinctiveness of a college and its programs. Generally, the focus of institutional impact studies has been to determine economic gains to the community produced by attending a community college, the social value of having a community college, and/or the gains to the individual in learning, earning, and performance (Linthicum, 1982). Richard Alfred (1982, pp. 93-94) has suggested that institutional impact studies should answer these six questions:

1. What are the effects of two-year college degree and nondegree programs on individual earnings, employment, and social development?

2. What are the cost benefits to business and industry of labor development programs offered in community colleges?

3. Do states and localities experience direct economic benefits as a result of community college programs?

4. What are the social and economic benefits to agencies of government—national, state, and local—associated with investment in community college education?

5. Does the community college education improve the quality of life through absorption of unemployed and indigent groups in the population?

6. What is the relationship of community college programs to economic development in a recessionary economy?

While all six of Alfred's questions attempt to place the community college in relation to the larger social, economic, and political communities it serves, no comparative data are generated. Institutional impact studies audit the role the college plays relative to its costs to constituencies. While needs assessments focus on the social and psychological needs for learning and marketing studies explore the values and attitudes of the public toward the institution, impact studies use economic modes of inquiry in order to explore social-institutional interaction. As such, impact studies add one more means of probing the unique qualities of the college. Unfortunately, those qualities cannot be applied comparatively, for other colleges and universities may have a different set of data, gathered using divergent procedures and demonstrating a comparable impact or impacts on local constituents.

Marketing Studies. Marketing studies have as their intent the organization of program, procedures, and publicity so as to bring about "voluntary exchanges of values with target markets for the purposes of achieving organizational objectives" (Kotler, 1975, p. 5). Marketing programs normally focus on the educational program, process, or image of the college. A carefully constructed marketing study can uncover that which is distinctive about a college and that which is not.

Like needs assessments, marketing studies may rely on surveys of various groups. Businesses may be asked what is the image of the college as a provider of training, alumni may be asked what was the educational climate on campus for learning, or employers may be asked what are the strengths and weaknesses of specific college programs in providing qualified workers. Marketing studies, however, also use interviews and focus groups as means of determining college image. The purpose of interviews and focus groups is not to gather a representative sample of views about the college; rather, they are intended to compile a comprehensive assessment of the values held by the market group toward the product, process, or image of the college.

Marketing studies tend to be point-in-time information-gathering activities from a specific group or groups. Questions are posed to a number of individuals from a target group, and the validity of the investigation hinges on the perceptions of the individuals surveyed or interviewed (Boatwright and Crowley, 1987). The information gathered does not provide corroboration of findings outside the group surveyed.

Strategic Planning Studies. Strategic planning consists of a family of planning procedures used to determine what decisions are appropriate to the college today based on information about the internal values of the college and its staff and the external forces impinging on its future. Strategic planning assumes that the college is an open system that is dynamic and reflexive to changes in a turbulent external environment. Strategic planning procedures, then, examine the connections between college and constituents, as well as between college and macro trends, such as technological or demographic change (Cope, 1981; Morrison, Renfro, and Boucher, 1984). Through this type of examination, the college has the opportunity to explore its unique qualities and relationships with its constituencies.

Central to the information-gathering portion of strategic planning is a process called environmental scanning. Through this process, the planning group decides on sources of pertinent information regarding external trends in a variety of areas potentially impacting the college: political, demographic, economic, social, technological, and competitive trends and forces. This information is then used to determine possible threats to the college operation and potential opportunities on which the college may wish to capitalize. Through the extrapolation of future trends, issues, and forces, the college's distinct and unique relationship to its environment is identified, and college goals and direction are given.

Morrison, Renfro, and Boucher (1984) have given detailed lists of information sources to be used and procedures to be followed in environmental scanning. Guiding the scanning process is a taxonomy of information sources, such as those used by the Trends Analysis Program of the American Council of Life Insurance. Here the principal sources of information are popular journals and newspapers, such as the *Wall Street Journal, Atlantic Monthly,* and *Science and Public Policy.* In short, environmental scanning relies heavily on secondary sources to form a profile of future forces, factors, and trends. Validation comes from recurring mention of a given factor or force. Triangulation (Mathison, 1988) of three or more categories of sources of a trend or issue is also used as a basis for validating the projections.

Conclusion

Institutional histories focus on persevering traditions, trends, and critical incidents that may contribute to the unique identity of the institution; the focus allows a view from past to present. Impact studies tend to rely on follow-up, economic, and demographic data; as such, the view of the institution is over a shorter and more recent time frame. Needs assessments and marketing studies are usually confined to the immediate; data are gathered from current clientele and student groups, and their perceived needs, interests, and attitudes toward the college are examined. Strategic planning disposes the researcher to examine the future; because environmental scanning focuses on external forces, future trends, and emerging issues, the information gathered is often of a more speculative nature.

Each of these data-gathering and analytic activities can unearth specific information about institutional distinctiveness. None of these will do so unless the study, the history, or the plan is specifically structured to gather reliable information about the college's identity. Each of these activities has a different time frame, information base, and perspective; therefore none alone will provide a comprehensive portrait of institutional distinctiveness. Yet a combination of these major data-gathering activities can be used to verify, and make the case for institutional distinctiveness. Given the increased data that are gathered to satisfy federal, state, and local agencies, the identity seeker would be prudent to use those data as sources rather than to begin data gathering afresh.

Regardless of what combination of sources is used, one individual or a central committee should be responsible for examining the institutional identity and should thus monitor the collection and use of information from other college institutional research efforts. The information gathered through the various studies and plans of the college can then be supplemented, where needed, with additional evidence to ensure the validity and strength of the individual's or the committee's argument for distinctiveness.

This chapter began with Delbert Brunton, who lost his job in 1916 because he didn't fully understand the unique attachment of the community to Fullerton Junior College. A contemporary institution, Northeast Iowa Technical Institute, was also seen to be threatened by a legislator over a question of institutional distinctiveness. These specific examples demonstrate that the quest for college identity should receive high priority, commitment from the president, and an appropriate allocation of time and resources from the organization. It should not be a secondary activity. Rapid social, economic, and technological changes demand effective responses and educational leadership from community colleges. Only with valid, reliable, and convincing information can the case for distinctiveness of mission and function be made.

References

Alfred, R. L. "Improving College Resources Through Impact Assessment." In R. L. Alfred (ed.), *Institutional Impacts on Campus, Community, and Business Constituencies.* New Directions for Community Colleges, no. 38. San Francisco: Jossey-Bass, 1982.

Boatwright, J., and Crowley, J. "A 1980s Approach to Planning: The Houston Community College System." In W. W. Wilms and R. W. Moore (eds.), *Marketing Strategies for Changing Times.* New Directions for Community Colleges, no. 60. San Francisco: Jossey-Bass, 1987.

Cope, R. *Strategic Planning, Management, and Decision Making.* AAHE-ERIC Higher Education Research Report no. 9. Washington, D.C.: American Association for Higher Education, 1987.

Eells, W. C. *Bibliography on Junior Colleges.* Office of Education Bulletin, no. 2. Washington, D.C.: U.S. Government Printing Office, 1930.

Goldman, E. F. *Rendezvous with Destiny.* New York: Random House, 1956.

Hofstader, R. *Age of Reform.* New York: Random House, 1955.

Kotler, P. *Marketing for Nonprofit Organizations.* Englewood Cliffs, N.J.: Prentice-Hall, 1975.

Library of Congress. *Newspapers on Microform, 1914–1972.* Washington, D.C.: U.S. Government Printing Office, 1976.

Linthicum, D. S. "Does Community College Education Produce Changes in Students?" In R. L. Alfred (ed.), *Institutional Impacts on Campus, Community, and Business Constituencies.* New Directions for Community Colleges, no. 38. San Francisco: Jossey-Bass, 1982.

Mathison, S. "Why Triangulate?" *Educational Researcher,* 1988, *17* (2), 13–17.

Morrison, J. L., Renfro, W. L., and Boucher, W. I. *Futures Research and Implications for Higher Education.* ASHE-ERIC Higher Education Research Report no. 9. Washington, D.C.: Association for the Study of Higher Education, 1984.

Plummer, L. E. *A History of the Fullerton Union High School and Fullerton Junior College, 1893–1943.* Fullerton, Calif.: Fullerton Junior College Press, 1949.

Ratcliff, J. L. "'First' Public Junior Colleges in an Age of Reform." *Journal of Higher Education,* 1987a, *57,* 151–180.

Ratcliff, J. L. *NITI Needs Assessment Study: A Study of the Postsecondary Educational Needs of Merged Area I.* Ames, Iowa: Higher Education Section, Iowa State University, 1987b. (ED 287 541)

Read, S. H. *The Green Child.* New York: New Directions, 1948.

Reid, A. E. "A History of the California Public Junior College Movement." Unpublished doctoral dissertation, University of Southern California, 1966.

Strobel, E. C., Jr. "Wayne County Community College: A History of Its Antecedents, Establishment, and Early Development in the Metropolitan Detroit Setting." Unpublished doctoral dissertation, Wayne State University, 1975.

James L. Ratcliff is professor and section leader of higher education at Iowa State University.

A community college can best utilize research on institutional distinctiveness when it is related to the college's particular stage of organizational development and when research findings are integrated with strategic planning and decision-making processes.

Using What an Institution Learns in the Search for Distinctiveness

Robert G. Templin, Jr.

What is it that our community college does? What should it be doing? What is our institution good at doing? What is it that we are known for in our community? How are we different from other educational institutions? What are the essential characteristics that distinguish us as a community college? What is unique about what we do? Answers to such questions are essential for educational institutions in today's rapidly changing world. Community colleges that have no clear idea of how to approach these types of questions will find it increasingly difficult to adapt, let alone thrive, in the future. One of the ways to approach these and related questions is to think about a community college's distinctive qualities or characteristics that define it as an educational institution. Research methodologies previously described in this volume can be invaluable in aiding an institution's search for distinctiveness.

Doing research on institutional distinctiveness, however, can be a wasted effort unless the results are connected to decisions considered essential to the welfare of the college. The quest for institutional distinctiveness for its own sake, no matter how intrinsically interesting, is probably of the same questionable worth as chasing students for the sake of

B. K. Townsend (ed.). *A Search for Institutional Distinctiveness.*
New Directions for Community Colleges, no. 65. San Francisco: Jossey-Bass, Spring 1989.

enrollment growth alone. It is only within the broader context of a college's organizational development, its mission and goals, and strategic planning processes that institutional distinctiveness takes on its full meaning. It is only as we connect the research results to action that the full potential of the concept is revealed. Consequently, discussion of how an institution uses what it has learned in its research on distinctiveness must be tied to the broader context of institutional concerns.

Stages of Organizational Development

What use a college makes of research on its distinctiveness has a lot to do with its particular stage of organizational development. In his work on organizational renewal, Gordon Lippitt (1969) suggested at least three developmental stages of organizational growth, with the stages arranged in a hierarchy similar to Maslow's "hierarchy of needs" (Maslow, 1954). According to Lippitt, the predominant issue being faced by an organization at any given time depends on the stage of development toward which it is moving. If the organization is in a primitive developmental stage, critical concern might well focus on survival. At a more fully developed stage, however, the dominant concern could involve achieving stability, gaining a reputation, or developing pride. If the organization is reaching toward maturity, then its critical issues might be how to achieve uniqueness and how to contribute more broadly to society.

Applying Lippitt's concept to community colleges, we can see that, if an institution has recently undergone a steady enrollment drop followed by faculty and staff layoffs and a sense of a worsening crisis, then identifying its distinctiveness may consist of determining what the defining characteristics of the college are or what the essential institutional characteristics are that make it needed as a college in the community. For a stable institution that has a clear sense of mission and is tending toward strengthening and integrating its programs and services, then the issue of distinctiveness may focus on the question, "What are the defining strengths of this college on which we shall build our reputation and our integrity?" For the mature institution striving toward "self-actualization," the issue of distinctiveness may revolve around defining the unique character of the college. All these different questions are related to the quest for distinctiveness, and all are appropriate, given the right match between the quest and the college's stage of development.

Strategic Planning and Decision Making

The richest potential application of research results about a college's distinctive characteristics is likely to be in the arena of strategic management and planning. It is through these processes that knowledge of a college's real and perceived distinctive character or potential can be woven into the institution's future direction.

Myran (1983) defines strategic management for community colleges as "a future-creating process that guides and integrates the various strategies and decisions of the college in such a way that the college as a whole is positioned favorably in relation to emerging opportunities and threats in the external environment" (p. 11). Essential to this process is an assessment of the ways in which the external environment is likely to change and then impact the college. Some changes are likely to present opportunities for the college in the form of emerging educational needs. Other trends, such as changing demographics, are likely to present problems, such as declining numbers in certain segments of the population that the college has traditionally served. Both opportunities and problems need to be anticipated and the college strategically positioned to its best advantage. But how does an institution decide how to "strategically position itself," and how does the college consider what is to its "best advantage"?

One of the best ways for colleges to begin to answer such questions is by incorporating research results on institutional distinctiveness within the broader context of strategic planning. Strategic planning studies that assess the external environment and ways that educational needs are changing should incorporate considerations of how an institution, its faculty, programs, and traditions are distinctively suited to a given set of emerging educational needs. What makes the concept of distinctiveness so useful within strategic planning is that it requires answering the question of institutional capability in relation to external conditions. This type of internal auditing permits a look at the institution and what it might be tomorrow in relation to what it stands for today. In addition to anticipating what the emerging educational needs of the community may be, the college must know whether those needs are appropriate to its current distinctive character and to what it is becoming. One of the first steps in this process recommended by nearly all writers on strategic management is that a college seek answers to the questions, "What is our mission, role, and scope?" and "What should be our mission, role, and scope?" (Cope, 1981, p. 3).

Because of the growing tendency during the 1960s and 1970s for community colleges to try to be all things to all people, and because many four-year colleges have adopted open-admissions policies and admitted large numbers of part-time and adult students, it has become increasingly difficult for the public and indeed for faculty and administrators themselves to identify the distinctive mission of the community college. One result has been a general lack of public understanding regarding the role of the American community college in today's society. George Vaughan (1986), in his extensive study of the community college presidency, cited as a major research finding, that "the perceived overwhelming failure of the community college has been the unwillingness or inability of its leaders to interpret and articulate its mission effectively, thereby failing to present consistently a positive image to its various publics" (p. 108).

Having a clear idea of the college's mission and how it is likely to be pursued in the midst of a changing environment permits one to relate research findings on distinctiveness to an image of the college not only as it is now but also as it is likely to be in the future. Several potential applications in this regard could be particularly useful to the college's leadership. These include developing a shared vision for the college around which others can rally, marketing the college, creating and communicating a positive image of the college among both internal and external constituents, interrelating college programs, and facilitating the development of institutional integrity.

Building a Shared Vision for the College. In his book on the college presidency, James Fisher (1984) stresses the importance of leaders developing a vision for the college so as to provide a focal point around which those within the institution can rally: "Although important for all, a special presidential vision is especially important for small, liberal arts colleges and regional public institutions (two- and four-year). Within such situations, people need a more significant collective identity, a sense of pride that tends to inspire both new heights and sacrifices for a greater cause" (p. 58).

Armed with knowledge about the institution's empirical and perceived distinctive characteristics, college leaders may use these research results as a springboard for constructing a shared vision that helps to define what the institution stands for, how those who commit themselves to the institution's mission are committing themselves to a distinctive cause, and why being associated with the college is part of a special calling.

Marketing the Institution. Marketing is a concept often confused with the external selling of the institution. According to Cope (1981), "marketing, as part of strategic planning, is intended to assist institutions in choosing the best match between what they can offer and the needs of their constituents" (pp. 35–37). Knowing in what ways the college is attempting to develop distinctiveness, especially if this is part of a strategic process, permits the college to position itself favorably with regard to emerging educational needs and to develop a comparative advantage over other colleges and universities. Emerging educational needs are assessed against the mission of the institution and its distinctive qualities in an effort to establish a market niche.

Creating and Communicating a Positive Institutional Image. This task should become more manageable as a college better defines for itself what it perceives as its distinctive elements. External relations can be guided as emerging institutional qualities and elements are identified and given priority. Publications can be developed with themes that promote the distinctive dimensions of the college. The total public relations program should develop greater coherence and organization as a result of establishing priorities about how the community college plays a distinctive role or provides a distinctive experience. By applying research results, the institution's "image makers" should be able to represent the institution in a way that reinforces perceptions shared by faculty and staff themselves, rather than promoting an image that to insiders appears to be only so much hype.

Interrelating College Programs. Research findings about an institution's distinctiveness should be helpful not just on the institutional level but also on the programmatic level. The ways in which curricula and services contribute to the institution's distinctive character should be one criterion used in program evaluation and at budget time when considering special funding aspects for strengthening programs. Similarly, new programs should be reviewed based on how they will promote the college's quest for distinctiveness. Simply having or adding programs that have unique features does not necessarily contribute to an institution's distinctive character. More important is how programs with distinctive elements are interrelated to contribute to greater programmatic coherence within the institution, thereby creating a distinctive theme or pattern that distinguishes the college from others. Starting a new program in aerospace robotics technology may do little for the institution's development of distinctiveness unless the program also can be related to a larger institutional theme, such as a broad commitment of programs and services to the aerospace industry.

Facilitating Institutional Integrity. Research on institutional distinctiveness can play a crucial role in the development of institutional integrity by helping to define and maintain the core character and values of the college in the midst of a potentially turbulent external environment. It is within the broader context of strategic planning that such research serves as a form of internal assessment. What makes the institution distinctive as seen from the insider's perspective has to be reconciled with how the institution is perceived from the public's point of view and with empirical research results. What should emerge eventually is a closer coalescence between what many think the college should be and what it is in reality. What those within an institution think the college is should be compared with the changing external environment to see how well the two match. Insights gained from this comparison can be used to raise new questions about the future. As Keller (1983) writes: "While an institution's own hopes and the outside forces of history are not exactly 'opposed,' anyone planning strategically for a college, school, or university needs to keep two incongruous bodies of facts and ideas—internal aspirations and external conditions—in mind at the same time and act to move the institution ahead nevertheless" (p. 145).

The Two-Edged Sword of Distinctiveness

The decision to apply research results on a college's distinctiveness must be made with the awareness that internal and external (or public) perceptions of distinctiveness provide both opportunities and problems. Once an institution becomes widely reputed as having a particular distinctive characteristic, such a reputation may well limit the kinds of initiatives the public or the faculty will consider appropriate to the college's "tradition."

It is essential that an institution's distinctive qualities be taken into account as major policy or mission changes are considered. For example, if a technical institute decides to expand its mission by becoming a comprehensive community college, it will gain new opportunities for service to the community but at a likely cost of diffusing its perceived distinctiveness. The intended purpose may be to expand services, but the unintended consequences might well be a blurring of the institutional identity in the eyes of the community, college members, and supporters.

Ideally, developing institutional distinctiveness involves working with elements that are in a core area or are central to the college's mission. But that is not always easy to do. Sometimes achieving distinctiveness requires beginning a new program, function, or service that, although indeed distinctive, may initially be regarded as only peripherally related to the college's main thrust. The danger of pursuing a distinctive element perceived to be unrelated to the centrality of the mission is that, during times of crisis or financial stress, that element may be seen as an unreasonable burden to the college's core programs or services. Pursuing distinctiveness may come to be seen as an unworthy effort that disproportionately consumes scarce resources and contributes to the college's predicament. Rather than serving as a rallying point for the college, such distinctive programs become symbols of poor judgment and bad management.

Projecting a distinctive image to the public can also be a two-edged sword. In the minds of some, an image of what a college is also leads to inferring what a college is not. By virtue of being known as low-cost, open-door institutions, community colleges are also assumed to be low quality. By offering an array of distinctive technical programs, some colleges may be regarded as "good technical schools" but not "real colleges." Having attempted to define more explicitly what the institution is about, one runs the risk of having the public perceive also what it is not in ways unintended by college leadership.

References

Cope, R. *Strategic Planning, Management, and Decision Making.* AAHE-ERIC Higher Education Research Report no. 9. Washington, D.C.: American Association for Higher Education, 1981.

Fisher, J. L. *Power of the Presidency.* New York: American Council on Education/Macmillan, 1984.

Keller, G. *Academic Strategy: The Management Revolution in American Higher Education.* Baltimore, Md.: Johns Hopkins University Press, 1983.

Lippitt, G. L. *Organization Renewal: Achieving Vitality in a Changing World.* New York: Appleton-Century-Crofts, 1969.

Maslow, A. H. *Motivation and Personality.* (1st ed.) New York: Harper & Row, 1954.

Myran, G. A. "Strategic Management in the Community College." In G. A. Myran (ed.), *Strategic Management in the Community College.* New Directions for Community Colleges, no. 44. San Francisco: Jossey-Bass, 1983.

Vaughan, G. B. *The Community College Presidency.* New York: American Council on Education/Macmillan, 1986.

Robert G. Templin, Jr., is president of Thomas Nelson Community College in Hampton, Virginia.

The benefits to a community college of undergoing a search for institutional distinctiveness include increased morale of institutional members and an improved image within the local community.

Benefits of Conducting a Search for Institutional Distinctiveness

Barbara K. Townsend

The benefits of a search for institutional distinctiveness occur in three stages: (1) the initial benefits resulting from undergoing the search itself, (2) the further benefits derived from learning the results of the search, and (3) the benefits gained from using the results of the search.

Benefits of Undergoing the Search

When community college leaders decide to conduct a search for institutional distinctiveness, they are indicating, both to internal and external constituents, a commitment to institutional evaluation. Such a commitment is vitally needed in the community college, for too often those within the institution have shied away from an honest appraisal of it. Troubled by charges of being "second best" (Zwerling, 1976) and of "cooling out" students who aspire to careers that others deem inappropriate for them (Clark, 1960), community college administrators and faculty also face being considered inferior by some in academia for working with students who often have marginal academic skills. With their institution assailed for not being like a more selective four-year one, many within

B. K. Townsend (ed.). *A Search for Institutional Distinctiveness.*
New Directions for Community Colleges, no. 65. San Francisco: Jossey-Bass, Spring 1989.

the community college have reacted defensively, maintaining that everything they do is right because their efforts are for the right reason—to provide an education to those who would not normally receive one. Hiding behind good intentions, those within the community college have frequently failed to evaluate candidly their own institution, both as a sector of higher education and as a specific institution.

While few senior-level administrators have either the time or the inclination to enter into national debates about the value of the community college, most of these administrators are concerned about the worth of their own particular college. One approach to determining its value is to conduct an institutional evaluation. A certain kind of evaluation takes place periodically when a college conducts a self-study as part of the accreditation process, but such a process is motivated by an external agency. In addition, the self-study is often conducted with an eye toward correcting or even hiding weaknesses rather than uncovering unknown strengths. Conducting a search for institutional distinctiveness is another way to evaluate an institution. Since the decision to conduct such a search is made voluntarily and not at the impetus of accrediting bodies or state agencies, it indicates a clear commitment on the part of institutional leaders to have their institution be the best that it can be. By deciding to conduct a search, leaders signal to faculty, staff, and students as well as to community members that determining the institution's strengths and weaknesses is "standard operating procedure" in leading the institution.

As well as indicating their commitment to evaluation, institutional leaders send out another message to internal constituents by deciding to search for distinctiveness. Since part of the search process involves ascertaining internal constituents' perceptions of the college, these constituents receive the message that their perceptions are important to the college's senior-level administration. Belief that one's thoughts and feelings matter to those who are in charge improves morale and contributes to a stronger commitment to the institution.

Conducting an assessment of the institution's strengths and weaknesses is also one of the first steps in the strategic planning process of developing and maintaining a "fit" between the institution and the market (Kotler and Murphy, 1981). As Robert Templin indicated in Chapter Six, a major use of a search for institutional distinctiveness is for strategic planning, the adoption of which has been strongly endorsed for successful management of institutions (Cope, 1981; Keller, 1983; Masoner and Essex, 1986–87; Myran, 1983). As part of strategic planning, senior-level administrators in community colleges need to take inventory of their institution's assets, such as its facilities and people, and ascertain its distinctive elements. In so doing, they gain a better understanding of their institution's possibilities and limitations. This understanding will help them determine the college's appropriate educational niche in the

local community. Deciding to conduct a search for institutional distinctiveness, in the manner described in this book, demonstrates a commitment to strategic planning, for the search will yield much of the
information needed for this process.

Benefits of Learning the Results of the Search

When the results of the search are made known, institutional leaders
may make several discoveries. They may find that there is little, if anything, that is distinctive about their particular community college. As
unsettling as this discovery may be, it can be beneficial. It may help
explain why the institution's enrollment has been declining while that
of a nearby state college, similar to the community college in many of its
functions but distinctive in the image it projects, has been increasing.
Even if the community college's current enrollment is stable, discovering
that the institution lacks much distinctiveness may alert institutional
leaders to the potential for an enrollment problem if local residents have
no other reason to choose XXX Community College over YYY State
College or ZZZ Proprietary School except that of cost. Lack of distinctive
institutional elements and capabilities is a serious detriment in today's
fierce institutional competition for students.

A far more desired result is the discovery that a particular community
college has several empirically distinctive programs and is perceived by
both internal and external constituents to be distinctive on some dimensions considered vital to the learning process. Institutional leaders can
then be assured of the worth of their institution in the local arena of
higher education institutions. The leaders, however, must be careful not
to rest content with this knowledge but must strive to maintain the distinctive programs deemed economically viable and to encourage further
internal and external support for the dimensions perceived as distinctive.

Another discovery may be that perceptions of internal constituents
and external constituents do not jibe. For example, faculty and academic
administrators may pride themselves on their transfer programs only to
learn that those outside the institution believe these programs are inferior
to the equivalent general education offerings of the local state college or
private university. If this difference in perception were not discovered,
the institution's faculty and administrators would lack the impetus to
reexamine the curriculum and the teaching-learning process in order to
discover ways to strengthen the academic programs and improve their
image in the minds of community members. Institutional leaders might
also discover that, while those within the community college may pride
themselves on their constant efforts to develop innovative programs, both
academic and support services, those outside the community may be
unaware of the college's innovative efforts or may even be hostile to

them out of educational conservatism or fear of rising college costs. Since the ultimate goal of a search for institutional distinctiveness is the congruence between internal and external views of the institution, it is extremely beneficial for a community college's leaders to learn of any major discrepancies in these two groups' views.

Benefits of Using the Results of the Search

A common complaint about evaluation is that it requires a lot of work, yet its results are seldom used. During accreditation studies, many institutions almost put their internal workings on hold while institutional members conduct the required self-study. Yet the results of the self-study are often not shared with faculty and staff and sometimes seem to go unheeded by administrators.

It is not enough to learn what, if anything, is distinctive about a particular community college. Institutional leaders must use this information, not merely disseminate it internally and then dismiss it as "interesting" but "irrelevant" to the everyday management of the community college.

The information derived in a search for institutional distinctiveness can be used in a variety of ways to benefit the institution both internally and externally:

First, the search for institutional distinctiveness may reveal that the institution has several distinctive programs and capabilities of which the college can be proud. When this information is shared with faculty and staff, one benefit may be their increased appreciation for their institution. Learning that the college in which one works has several distinctive features is likely to contribute to one's sense of pride in the institution and to a more positive sense of identification with it. An improved external image may, in turn, result when these internal constituents verbalize to their family and friends their pride in the institution.

Second, students' morale can be improved as they, too, learn that their institution is noteworthy for certain academic elements. Not only will they have increased pride in attending XXX Community College but this increased pride may also result in other benefits to the institution. Students who are proud of the institution they attend make good recruiters of other students. Also, for community colleges whose operating budget derives partly from local funding, students who are impressed with the institution may be inclined to vote for increases in local funding for the institution. Finally, once the students become alumni, they may also be more inclined to make financial contributions.

Third, if the results of the search should be "negative"—that is, if they reveal that there is little, if anything, that is distinctive about the college—this information can be used with internal constituents (faculty and staff) for the institution's benefit. For example, it may be revealed that the general education curriculum is little more than a pastiche of courses yielding no curricular coherence. Such a revelation can be used to motivate the faculty to commit itself to reworking the curriculum so that it becomes a distinctive institutional feature rather than a mere smorgasbord of courses. Similarly, conflicting perceptions about institutional features may result in improvement of specific ones. If faculty feel that they are caring individuals in the classroom but learn that students and/or external constituents do not perceive them in the same way, the faculty need to reexamine their classroom behavior. After doing so, they may decide that the behavior is entirely appropriate but simply misunderstood by students. Faculty could then endeavor to explain their actions to students as part of the classroom interaction.

Fourth, use of the results of a search for institutional distinctiveness should ultimately result in an improved image in the local community once the college's distinctive elements are identified or developed and then clearly and consistently conveyed. If this occurs, enrollment gains are highly probable. For example, as community members who desire enrollment in a particular program learn that XXX Community College is the only local institution where this program is offered, enrollment in it should increase. Similarly, if community members perceive that XXX Community College provides a distinctive dimension to the teaching-learning process, they may choose to enroll in the community college not only because it is less costly than other postsecondary institutions but also because they deem it to be the best.

Conclusion

An institution that has conducted a search for institutional distinctiveness can benefit in several major ways: (1) It can determine the areas in which it wants to be distinctive, (2) it can take steps to ensure distinctiveness in these areas, and (3) it can take steps to ensure that these distinctive elements are accurately represented to all its constituents, both internal and external. The ultimate benefit of a search for institutional distinctiveness should be an institution offering programs and services that both its internal and external constituents agree are valuable. When the perceptions of these groups are ascertained and brought into congruence, community college leaders will be able to develop and maintain their institution as a true "college of choice" (Eaton, 1987) within the local educational arena.

References

Clark, B. R. *The Open-Door College: A Case Study.* New York: McGraw-Hill, 1960.
Cope, R. *Strategic Planning, Management, and Decision Making.* AAHE-ERIC Higher Education Research Report no. 9. Washington, D.C.: American Association for Higher Education, 1981.

Eaton, J. "Overview: Colleges of Choice." In J. Eaton (ed.), *Colleges of Choice: The Enabling Impact of Community Colleges*. New York: American Council on Education/Macmillan, 1987.

Keller, G. *Academic Strategy: The Management Revolution in American Higher Education*. Baltimore, Md.: Johns Hopkins University Press, 1983.

Kotler, P., and Murphy, P. E. "Strategic Planning for Higher Education." *Journal of Higher Education*, 1981, *52* (5), 470–489.

Masoner, D. J., and Essex, N. L. "A Call for Strategic Planning: The Two-Year College Imperative." *Community College Review*, 1986-87, *14* (3), 31–35.

Myran, G. A. (ed.). *Strategic Management in the Community College*. New Directions for Community Colleges, no. 44. San Francisco: Jossey-Bass, 1983.

Zwerling, S. *Second Best: The Crisis of the Community College*. New York: McGraw-Hill, 1976.

Barbara K. Townsend is assistant professor of higher education at Loyola University of Chicago and is a former community college faculty member and administrator.

Triton College's search for institutional distinctiveness, assisted by an outside researcher, provided college constituencies with new insights about their institution.

Triton College: One Institution's Search for Distinctiveness

Barbara K. Townsend, James L. Catanzaro

While the preceding chapters have prescribed why and how leaders of a community college should conduct a search for institutional distinctiveness, readers may well question if this prescription or theory can translate into effective practice. This chapter recounts how the search for institutional distinctiveness was undertaken at Triton College in Illinois and what the results of the search were.

Triton's Background

Founded in 1964 as a junior college, Triton College is located in Chicago's western suburbs in the midst of residential and industrial developments. When the Illinois Public Community College System was established in 1965, Triton reorganized and became a comprehensive community college, part of a system that now has thirty-nine districts operating fifty comprehensive colleges and enrolling a headcount of over 320,000 students in the fall of 1987 (Illinois Community College Board, 1988). The system's colleges are funded primarily through state funds (in the form of Illinois Community College Board grants), local taxes, and student tuition and fees.

B. K. Townsend (ed.). *A Search for Institutional Distinctiveness.*
New Directions for Community Colleges, no. 65. San Francisco: Jossey-Bass, Spring 1989.

Encompassing sixty-three square miles with over 320,000 residents, Triton's district is one of the largest industrial centers in Illinois. With a fall 1987 student headcount of over 18,000 (over 13,000 of whom were part time), Triton is the second largest community college in Illinois and among the fifteen largest single-campus community colleges in the nation (Illinois Community College Board, 1988; Palmer, 1988). Because of its size and location in a major industrial center, Triton has become a leader in high-technology instruction. It is also known statewide for its strong continuing education programs for health professionals.

Steps in the Search

The decision to research systematically the distinctive elements and dimensions of Triton College was the serendipitous result of an outside researcher desiring to study the institution at the same time as a new president was assuming command of the college. New to Illinois and its system of community colleges, the president desired to learn as much as he could about Triton College. At the same time, a higher education professor at a nearby university desired to study the community college as a distinctive type of higher education institution. The approach she selected was to examine a particular community college, in this case Triton College, for its distinctive qualities and elements. When she contacted Triton's new president, he was receptive to her desire to determine Triton's distinctive elements and dimensions, since her data would assist him in understanding the nature of the institution he was now leading.

Accordingly, her search for the distinctive nature of Triton College was begun with the full support of the institution's president. Her presence on campus as a researcher was announced to campus constituencies through a memo to all personnel and through a write-up in a monthly Triton newsletter. In addition, she met with the administrative staff to explain the project and to ask for their cooperation and participation. The head of the faculty union was also contacted for the same reason.

Data were collected through interviews and document analysis. Those interviewed were selected for one or more reasons: their position within the college (for example, each dean was interviewed), availability, referral by another person being interviewed, or their requesting to be interviewed. A total of eighty-nine people were interviewed either in person or by phone: three members of the board of trustees; twenty-three administrators; nine middle managers; twelve classified staff; twenty-two faculty, including two part-timers; and twenty students.

The documents that were examined included institutional reports, brochures about academic programs and support services, student and institutional newsletters, and historical documents relating to the college's founding. Documents were readily available since the college has an archive and an office of institutional research.

Few problems were encountered in the data collection process. Some of those being interviewed initially expressed a concern about the confidentiality of their responses; however, they readily accepted the researcher's reassurance that she would be the only one to know who made what responses. Her being an outsider to the institution as well as someone who was doing the research in her role as a university professor rather than as a paid consultant seemed to reassure those being interviewed, who generally were quite open in their assessment of Triton's distinctive qualities, both positive and negative.

Conceptual Framework

In the search for Triton's institutional distinctiveness, two types of distinctiveness—empirical and perceived—were sought. As indicated in Chapter Three, empirical distinctiveness exists when there is tangible proof that an institution differs from other institutions on a particular element or dimension. Perceived distinctiveness occurs when elements or dimensions of an institution are thought by its constituents to be distinctive even though there may be little or no empirical reality to their perceptions.

Distinctiveness does not exist in a void. Stating that an institution is distinctive implies a comparison to other institutions that perform the same general functions. When educational leaders claim their college is distinctive, they may be claiming it is distinctive in comparison to other institutions of the same type, to other types of educational institutions, and/or to other educational institutions in their communty, their region, their state, or even the nation. Thus, when the president of a community college claims that her or his institution is distinctive, she or he may be saying it is distinctive in comparison to other community colleges, in comparison to four-year colleges and universities as well as proprietary schools, and/or in comparison to other higher or postsecondary education institutions in the community, service region, state, or nation.

To help focus the search for empirical and perceived distinctiveness when making these comparisons, the researcher established categories or areas that would serve as guidelines or parameters. The following ten, already delineated in Chapter Two, were used as the focusing categories: (1) institutional philosophy, (2) composition of the student body; (3) academic programs, (4) services, (5) delivery systems, (6) personnel, (7) organization, (8) facilities, (9) finances, and (10) community relations.

Triton's Empirical Distinctiveness

In several of these areas, it was readily apparent that Triton College was in no way distinctive nor did it attempt to be distinctive from other community colleges in its region, state, or in the nation. Its institutional philosophy is that of all community colleges in Illinois as well as community colleges generally: It is an open-door institution designed primarily to serve first-generation, lower-income, commuting students who live in its surrounding community (Cohen and Brawer, 1982). Thus, its admissions policy is open door and its cost to the student is low ($27 per credit hour in 1987–88 for in-district students).

Its student body is typical of many community colleges: predominantly white, part-time students in their late twenties (Cohen and Brawer, 1982; *Triton College Statistical Abstract 1987*), although over the last six years enrollment of minorities has gone from 10 to 23 percent. While Triton makes full use of such alternative modes of learning as the microcomputer and videotapes, its primary delivery system for instruction is the traditional one of the teacher speaking with students in a formal classroom setting.

Triton's personnel are similar demographically to other community college personnel, both in Illinois and in the nation (Cohen and Brawer, 1982; Illinois Community College Board, 1988). Its organization, finances, and community relations are also typical for community colleges in Illinois and in many states (Cohen and Brawer, 1982; Illinois Community College Board, 1988). It is atypical financially, however, in the amount of corporate support it receives: For 1986–87 Triton received the most corporate donations among public community colleges, receiving more than $3 million ("Triton Ranked Number One," 1988). Its facilities or buildings are typical of many community colleges (as well as many state four-year colleges) built in the 1960s: two-story concrete buildings set on several acres (in Triton's case, thirteen buildings on 110 acres).

It is in the area of academic programs that Triton achieves empirical distinctiveness. First of all, Triton is distinctive in the quantity of its program offerings. With 161 academic programs (20 of which are apprenticeship), it offers more programs than any other community college in its service region (Illinois Community College Board, 1988). It also offers more programs than do most community colleges nationally, although Miami–Dade Community College offers the most with 180 programs as of fall 1987 (Zwerling, 1988).

Quantity of program offerings is one dimension of programmatic distinctiveness, but there are others. The substance and structure of the academic programs or curricula also need to be evaluated for distinctiveness.

In terms of substance or content, Triton has a number of distinctive occupational-technical programs. These programs have always been an important part of Triton's image and identity: For many years Triton was known as the "Career Center of the Midwest" (Mohr, 1984). Currently it is the only community college in Illinois to offer seventeen of these programs, which include laser electro-optic technology, nuclear medicine technology, and waiter/waitress training. An additional nineteen occupational-technical programs are unique community college programs for its service region (Illinois Community College Board, 1988). Some of these programs cover greenhouse operation and management, robotics technology, tool and die making, and small engine repair. These same programs are also unique for nonprofit higher education institutions within its local area.

Sometimes an institution's academic programs are not distinctive in substance or content but may be distinctive in structure. Bergquist, Gould, and Greenberg (1981, p. 5) have devised a taxonomy of variables in curricular structure. Their taxonomy, which follows, was used in examining the structure of Triton's academic programs.

1. *Time:* Duration and schedule of instructional units
2. *Space:* Use of instructional and noninstructional areas both on and off the college campus
3. *Resources:* Instructional use of people, situations, and materials, both on and off campus, from instructional and noninstructional areas
4. *Organization:* Arrangement and sequencing of instructional units and arrangement of academic administrative units
5. *Procedures:* Planning, implementing, evaluating, and crediting instructional units
6. *Outcomes:* Defining the intended desired results of a particular instructional unit or academic program.

Of all higher education institutions, the community college has been the most flexible and creative in its handling of curricular time and space. Triton is no exception. While the majority of its courses are offered on a semester basis, Triton also offers other scheduling options, such as eight-week condensed courses, flexible entrance courses for courses organized into self-paced learning modules, and the Weekend College for those who wish to complete a degree in certain programs by attending only on weekends. The majority of Triton courses, no matter when they are offered, are offered on campus, either in a traditional classroom setting or in a lab appropriate to the course content. Like most community colleges, however, Triton does offer classes at extention centers such as area high schools.

As a community college Triton is not distinctive in its flexible scheduling of time and space. It is, however, distinctive on these dimensions in comparison to the area four-year colleges and universities and proprietary institutions that are its competitors for students. None of them provide as many schedule options or off-campus sites as Triton does.

Like most community colleges, Triton is versatile in its use of curricular resources. Thus, it draws heavily on people from local businesses and industries to serve as adjunct faculty in many of its occupational-technical programs. More significantly, in its degree and certificate programs, it has several agreements with regional industries such as Ford Motor Corporation to train employees on site. These on-site facilities contain the latest in equipment for the particular industry; thus, they represent valuable curricular resources for Triton.

Deviating from traditional curricular approaches on the structural dimensions of organization, procedures, and outcomes requires more far-reaching institutional changes than do deviations in time, space, and resources. Thus, it is not surprising that Triton is not distinctive from other community colleges or from most four-year colleges and universities nationally in its handling of these dimensions. Organizationally, Triton's instructional offerings in its degree programs follow the dominant model in higher education: concentration or major, general education, and electives. Its procedures for planning, implementing, evaluating, and crediting instructional units also follow the dominant models. The degree or certificate program is basically designed by the faculty and institution, and academic credit is attained primarily by completing successfully the required instructional units. Student performance is assessed in individual courses with no global assessment made during or on completion of a program. If specified, educational outcomes are delineated on a course-by-course basis rather than on a programmatic or institutional basis.

In sum, over a fifth of Triton's academic program offerings are empirically distinctive in substance: Triton is either the only community college within the state or within its service region to offer these programs. In addition, most of its academic programs are not offered at four-year colleges or universities since the programs are two years or less in length. Thus, Triton can easily and accurately claim some distinctiveness in program content or substance among community colleges and four-year colleges and universities in its region and state.

Triton can less accurately claim distinctiveness in terms of curricular structure. As a community college, it is more flexible than most four-year colleges and universities, both locally and nationally, on the curricular dimensions of time, space, and resources. But other community colleges in its service region as well as in Illinois and the nation have time and spatial arrangements similar to Triton's and also use community members and materials as instructional resources. On the more "profound" (Bergquist, Gould, and Greenberg, 1981) structural dimensions of organization, procedures, and outcomes, Triton is indistinguishable from most institutions of higher education, whether they be community colleges, four-year colleges, or universities.

Academic programs are not the only ones that can be assessed for institutional distinctiveness. As do all higher education institutions, Triton offers a variety of support services and programs to assist students in their academic endeavors. For example, Triton provides variable tuition rates in three ways: First, students eligible for honors sections of courses receive a tuition waiver for them. Second, students willing to take afternoon classes receive a 33 percent tuition reduction to encourage their enrollment during "off" hours. Finally, Triton has what it calls the Program Completion Incentive, whereby students who enroll in sophomore-level courses required for completion of an associate degree receive full tuition waivers. To encourage students to complete their associate degree and to fill upper-level classes, Triton offers this unique program, currently the only one of its kind among two- and four-year colleges and universities ("Triton Encourages Persistence," 1987). The Program Completion Incentive is an example of an empirically distinctive academic support service or program to which Triton can lay claim.

As a comprehensive community college, Triton offers not only academic transfer programs and occupational-technical programs with the concomitant support services but also devotes much of its energies to diverse continuing education efforts. For example, career development needs of community members are met through various short-term training programs, including ones for health professionals. An important part of this effort is the Employee Development Institute (EDI), which works with local businesses and industries and other community groups to arrange on-site training programs that develop employees both professionally and technically. While many community colleges currently have such a program, Triton's EDI was one of the first in the nation, having been part of Triton's School for Continuing Education for over fifteen years.

Thus, in addition to the empirical distinctiveness of some of its curricular offerings, Triton has several continuing education and support services programs that are or have been distinctive among the community colleges in its service area. Since they stem from the mission and nature of Triton as a community college, they are also distinctive activities and programs among local higher education institutions. For example, four-year colleges and universities, by virtue of their offering four-year programs, would not offer special financial incentives to complete the sophomore year of study.

Internal Constituents' Perceptions

While ascertaining what is empirically distinctive about a particular community college is an important part of that institution's search for distinctiveness, it is not the only part. It is equally important to learn how constituents within the institution perceive it.

To ascertain the perceptions of Triton's internal constituents about the distinctive elements of their institution, the outside researcher interviewed a number of them, either in person or by telephone. In the fall of 1987, the researcher asked eighty-nine internal constituents (board members, administrative staff, middle managers, classified staff, faculty, and students) to respond to the following question about Triton: "When you think about Triton College, what really stands out in your mind about the institution?" In addition, most of those interviewed were also asked what they would say about Triton if members of the community wanted to know why they should go there. This second question was asked as another way of ascertaining what internal constituents perceived as valuable about Triton.

When constituents' comments about Triton were examined, a number of elements emerged as distinctive in their perceptions. What was most outstanding in constituents' minds were the people who work at Triton. A typical response was, "There are a lot of good people working for Triton College. They are people oriented; they like dealing with the people, the public. People stay here because of the nice people they find here." Almost fifty positive comments were made about the faculty, who received praise from all constituencies for their quality, their qualifications, and their caring for students. Typical comments included the following:

- "We have very strong faculty here; very, very good teachers who know their disciplines well. They are doing research and are interested in media and technology."
- "There are a number of teachers here who really care that their students can think."
- "They seem to really care a great deal about their subject; they're not tired of teaching yet."
- "Faculty are very committed—they will go that one step further for parents and students."

Quite a few positive comments were also made about Triton's administration and staff (a term that was sometimes applied to all who work at Triton, including the faculty). Personnel other than faculty were described as "dedicated," "of very high caliber," "helpful," and with "students' interests at heart." The administration was praised for being "supportive," "willing to make decisions," and "good to work for." Comments about the administration were sometimes influenced by the recent arrival of a new president. Those who mentioned his arrival were quite optimistic about Triton's future with the new president. Sometimes specific groups of staff were praised. For example, students mentioned how advisers were "real friendly and helpful" and "really seem to be concerned."

While its personnel (faculty, staff, and administrators) were perceived as the most positive element by constituents, Triton's program diversity also was frequently mentioned: "In occupational-technical programs, Triton offers more than any community college in the state, maybe in the country." "There are incredible offerings—a lot of curriculums offered here are not offered at other colleges."

On the other hand, the fact that so many of its program offerings are in occupational-technical areas occasionally caused concern for Triton's academic image: "Triton is no better or worse than any community college. They are still perceived as high schools with ash trays. Triton College gets it [this image] because of its so many career programs. Only the dummies took vocational education in high school, so why would you go to our place which specializes in career education?"

Triton's low cost in comparison to other area colleges was also seen as a distinctive feature. Some viewed Triton's low cost as providing "a more cost-effective way to get transfer courses out of the way," while others saw the low cost as beneficial to parents, who "won't [have to] spend a fortune while Johnny is maturing or learning he doesn't want to go to college."

Not only would Johnny's parents not have to spend much for him to attend Triton but constituents also perceived that Johnny would be well treated while there. Triton was frequently perceived as being distinctive in its positive treatment of students. Typical comments included:

- "Students are offered direction—not merely set loose. They are offered direction through counseling, advising, and career development activities."
- "The student will get here what he will not get in larger universities. He will get the instructor's attention."
- "Students will see faculty with Ph.D.'s every day whereas in the university, you may see a Ph.D. only once a week."

Others cited "the tremendous potential for individual attention in classes," the "encouragement" by instructors, and the "personalized approach" in the classroom.

Another element frequently mentioned by those interviewed was Triton's campus, which was perceived to be very attractive, either in comparison to those of four-year colleges or other community colleges. Typical comments were: "The facilities are much more attractive than those of many four-year colleges," and "Our physical plant is unique. We look like a four-year university [sic]. We don't look like an office building or a bunch of Quonset huts in a cornfield, like many community colleges."

Constituents also noted the opportunities that Triton, as a community college, provides students and the local community: "Triton, as a community college, is good for the student because students wouldn't go [to college] otherwise. Its affordability and availability allow students a step up." "Triton seems to serve a very good community need. A lot of the people here were culturally deprived, and Triton College helps them culturally."

Board members seemed to be the most aware of this dimension of the institution, claiming distinctiveness for it because of its "opportunity . . . to adapt itself to changing needs in the community. It can identify needs and design programs to meet community needs." Board members also cited Triton as an institution that is "a center where people can meet for academic, social, and cultural reasons." Other constituents saw Triton's "community orientation" as distinctive because the institution "tries to reach out into the community and develop it, make . . . [its members] more aware, draw them into the college." As one respondent said, Triton is "community based. It is so integrated into the community. Everything goes into the soil. We grew from it and returned to it tenfold."

In addition, its members, particularly those in administration and middle management, perceived Triton as an institution whose administration encouraged staff members to be "innovative," "entrepreneurial," "creative," and "risk taking" and enabled them to be so by being "non-bureaucratic" and capable of "turning on a dime" or making a "quick response" to new ideas. Triton was also perceived as "aggressive in initiating state-of-the-art things" and always "seeking out the cutting edge." Occasionally the board of trustees' role in engendering this kind of climate was cited: "Triton is innovative because of . . . a board that more or less gave the administration free rein." "The board is very supportive of the college and basically allows the college to administer itself."

While an occasional classified staff or faculty member praised Triton for being "innovative" or "risk taking," constituents of these two groups were more apt to mention how "supportive" the institution or members of it were. For example, one faculty member said, "There is a lot of support for individual faculty members," while a classified staff member said, "The institution is supportive of you bettering yourself through education." Others spoke of the "encouragement" of new programs and offerings and of administrative support for innovations through the provision of released time and money.

In sum, what stands out positively about Triton College for its internal constituents is Triton's people (administration, staff, and faculty), its programmatic diversity, the benefits of attendance for students, its low cost, its attractive physical appearance, its relationship with the local community, and its supportive atmosphere for innovation and risk taking.

While constituents see these and others as distinctive aspects of Triton, some constituents also expressed reservations about Triton. Faculty sometimes mentioned concerns about the quality of students at Triton, as in the following comments:

- "Students here don't know how to go to school. . . . They don't have the commitment to quality work. Schoolwork is low on their priority list, after work, the opposite sex, etc. They don't invest in the future. Short-term gratification is more important."
- "Students lack the peer influence [there would be] at a better school."
- "Higher-level academic students aren't challenged here."

A few constituents expressed concern about Triton's tendency "to rest on its laurels," to place "emphasis on the sizzle rather than the substance," or "to stress quantity rather than quality." Several negative comments focused on the board of trustees and the political nature of Triton. In particular the relationship of the board to Triton was cited as being distinctive but not in a positive sense: "Triton has a very . . . unusual board relationship. Triton is very board driven—to the point of interference. There are tradeoffs. The administration can get travel money, etc., if the board gets its way, but this is not for the good of the institution." "As an institution, Triton is unusual because it seems to have such political overtones because of the board of trustees' effect on the college. Triton is managed from the outside through the board of trustees, which has a nonschool orientation and uses Triton as a political entity."

While politics and the board were often mentioned in the same breath, the political nature of the community and of Triton were also mentioned: "This is probably the most political school, at least in the Cook County community colleges—probably in the state. Why? Because Triton provides a lot of jobs for people—a place for politicians to get a lot of people working. It has politicians thinking, 'This is my college with contracts to be awarded and a budget of $32 million a year.'"

Evaluation of Triton's Distinctiveness

When Triton is compared to other community colleges, its empirical distinctiveness emerges as a manifestation of its size and financial resources. With its yearly headcount of over 18,000 students, Triton is among the fifteen largest single-campus community colleges in the nation. Its high headcount has been a factor in its receiving large amounts of state funding. In addition, Triton is fortunate to be in a state with a funding formula that enables community colleges to carry out their diverse functions. Also, the three communities that provide local funding for Triton are prosperous ones that have traditionally been supportive of providing funds for Triton. Equally important, the leadership at Triton has been both diligent and creative in searching out and obtaining resources, whether those resources be state and federal grants or equipment donations from local industry. Consequently, Triton has the financial resources to offer a wide variety of academic programs and innovative support services.

Because of its size and the consequent financial resources that stem from large size, Triton can afford to offer a wide range of occupational-technical programs. Within its service region and state, Triton is an empirically distinctive community college because of the large number of academic programs it offers. Nationally it joins the other large community colleges, such as Miami–Dade, in offering literally dozens of occupational-technical programs. Smaller community colleges simply cannot be distinctive in their *quantity* of program offerings as compared to institutions the size of Triton.

Triton can also afford to offer occupational-technical programs that have very high equipment costs. Programs such as robotics technology or laser electro-optic technology are not common offerings of most community colleges, partly because the equipment costs are too high. Thus, Triton achieves empirical distinctiveness in the *content* of many of its occupational-technical program offerings partly because it can afford the equipment costs.

Large size and abundant financial resources do not make for automatic distinctiveness in transfer programs. Community colleges that have achieved distinctiveness in these programs have usually done so through their requirements for the general education component of the associate of arts degree. For example, Kirkwood Community College has achieved national distinction, including praise from William Bennett (1984), with its revised general education program emphasizing the humanities. As indicated earlier, the requirements for Triton's associate of arts degree follow the standard distributive model in academia.

While its financial resources do not seem to have stimulated institutional members to develop a distinctive general education curriculum, the abundance of resources may be a factor in the physical attractiveness of the institution, especially its grounds. Although the architectural design of the buildings is not distinctive, the buildings are well kept. Attractive wood paneling and trim adorn much of the second floor of the building that houses the office of the president and those of some administrative staff. The wood paneling and trim are a legacy of Triton's first president, who believed in "going first class" (Frye, 1987) and had the financial resources to do so. The campus itself is nicely landscaped with well-tended grounds. Perceptions regarding the attractiveness of Triton are firmly based in reality. Less "real" or accurate may be perceptions that Triton is more attractive than other educational institutions, since empirical comparisons of this kind would be difficult to make.

Perceptions that Triton is providing opportunities for community members also seem well founded. As a community college, Triton is typical in its responsiveness to the needs of the communities it serves. While Triton College's name does not indicate that it is a community college, internal constituents' perceptions that Triton is intrinsically linked to its surrounding communities are well founded.

Among other types of higher education institutions, the main reference point for Triton's internal constituents was "the university." Constituents tended to compare Triton to "the university" and find the university lacking. For example, several Triton constituents indicated how Triton could better serve students than could "the university" because Triton students would be taught by faculty, not teaching assistants (TAs), and would receive more attention from instructors.

If one accepts the premises that TAs are not as effective instructors as regular faculty and that small classes lead to greater attention from instructors, then constituents' perceptions that Triton serves students better than does "the university" are correct. Because Triton is not a university, it does not have TAs in the classroom. All instructors, whether full or part time, have faculty rank. With an average on-campus class size of 19.3 (Illinois Community College Board, 1988), Triton's classes are small. They are small partly because the classrooms were built to accommodate no more than thirty-five students. By comparison, at the University of Illinois–Chicago, the state university that receives the largest number of transfers from Triton (McNerney, 1986a), classes for freshmen and sophomores may contain anywhere from 5 to 412 students, although the fall 1986 average for 100-level courses is 21.8 and 18.4 for 200-level courses (Nelson, 1988).

Triton constituents implied a comparison to all other types of educational institutions when they mentioned its low cost as one of its distinctive features. Constituents also perceived Triton to be distinctive in the attention students receive from faculty, at least in comparison to university faculty. These two features, however, may make Triton distinctive in comparison to other types of higher or postsecondary institutions but not in comparison to other community colleges. Traditionally, community colleges have been no- or low-cost institutions and have claimed to give students a great deal of academic attention (Cohen and Brawer, 1982).

In sum, Triton is empirically distinctive from many community colleges in the diversity of its academic programs, particularly in its occupational-technical programs. It also offers some support services that are distinctive or even unique for community colleges. A history of administrative support for innovation has resulted in the creation of some of these support services as well as of many community education activities. While its facilities are not architecturally unusual, they and the campus are perhaps distinctive in being well kept.

While Triton is perceived by its internal constituents as being distinctive among higher education institutions in the quality of its personnel, especially the faculty, there is no evidence to indicate that this perception is accurate. Another perception for which there is little empirical evidence is the belief that Triton faculty are more caring and provide more individual attention to students than do faculty at other higher education institutions, especially the university. Perhaps the existence of these perceptions is more important than their accuracy. Surely it is a plus for an institution if those who work within it believe that its personnel are outstanding and that the major service it provides, in this case faculty-student interaction, is better than that provided by institutions with a similar function. These perceptions help Triton's internal constituents to justify the existence and the value of their institution.

Potential Value of the Search to Triton

Much of the value of a search for distinctiveness is that it forces an institution to take a hard look at itself. For example, Triton now *knows* that some of its academic programs are distinctive in content or substance (that is, that no other area or regional or even state institution offers such programs) but that all of these distinctive programs are in occupational-technical areas. While it may be difficult for Triton to develop transfer programs that are distinctive in content because of the concern for transferability to four-year colleges and universities, Triton's leaders should consider applying the same sort of creative, innovative spirit to the content development of their transfer programs that they apply to their occupational-technical programs, support services, and other college activities.

An analysis of distinctiveness in curricular structure has also revealed that Triton's "innovative" efforts in curriculum development pertain primarily to the curricular dimensions of time and space, the ones least "profound" in nature. Those within Triton should consider if more fundamental structural changes can and should be made or if members are content to "tinker" with the curricula at the lowest levels of structural change.

Triton also needs to consider the drawbacks or the negative side to its support of entrepreneurialism and innovation. While many distinctive projects have resulted, a number of projects have failed, with little follow-up evaluation as to why. More important there has been no particular focus to the innovations. Instead, there has been a kind of scattershot approach that works against the creation of a distinctive element or dimension beyond that of global support of innovation.

Similarly, Triton's encouragement of a multiplicity of programs and services yields an institutional image of "something for everyone," the motto of community colleges in the 1970s. The downside to this approach is that not everything can be done well. Particularly since its enrollment is currently dropping, Triton may wish to consider pulling back from some of these activities, determining which ones it does particularly well and which are in demand by its service area, and focusing its efforts on these. In so doing, Triton may enhance its image for quality as well as quantity.

Triton should also check out the perceptions of its internal constituents with those of its external constituents. While Triton has conducted surveys of its image within the community in previous years (McNerney, 1986b), the purpose of these surveys has been merely to ascertain the perceptions of external constituents, not to gather these perceptions to compare them with those held by internal constituents. Those within Triton perceive its personnel to be outstanding and its students to receive greater faculty attention than do students at other colleges and universities. Since it is almost impossible to verify the accuracy of these perceptions, what matters is if members of the community hold similar ones. If they do, Triton should continue to emphasize these dimensions in its marketing of the institution. If external constituents do not hold similar perceptions of Triton personnel and/or of faculty-student interaction, Triton may wish to investigate the disparity between external and internal constituents' perceptions to determine if personnel changes need to be made or if classroom practices need to be altered.

This search for institutional distinctiveness has provided Triton with a better understanding of itself as an educational institution, both in comparison to other community colleges and in comparison to other sectors of higher education. Triton has found that its distinctiveness in comparison to many community colleges in Illinois and in the nation stems largely from its size and resources. Its distinctiveness in comparison to other sectors of higher education stems from its being a community college. Triton may well wish to harness its ethos of entrepreneurialism and innovation in order to focus on ways to strengthen further its best programs and services, perhaps eliminating the less effective ones. By so doing, Triton will find its distinctiveness based equally on quality and quantity.

References

Bennett, W. J. *To Reclaim a Legacy: A Report on the Humanities in Higher Education.* Washington, D.C.: National Endowment for the Humanities, 1984.

Bergquist, W. H., Gould, R. A., and Greenberg, E. M. *Designing Undergraduate Education: A Systematic Guide.* San Francisco: Jossey-Bass, 1981.

Cohen, A. M., and Brawer, F. B. *The American Community College.* San Francisco: Jossey-Bass, 1982.

Frye, J. (Executive director of personnel, Triton College.) Personal conversation with author, August 13, 1987.

Illinois Community College Board. *Data and Characteristics.* Springfield: Illinois Community College Board, 1988.

McNerney, N. *Colleges and Universities Triton Students Transferred to in Fall 1982, 1983, 1984, and 1985.* River Grove, Ill.: Office of Research and Analysis, Triton College, 1986a.

88

McNerney, N. *Survey of Triton's Image in the Community*. River Grove, Ill.: Office of Research and Analysis, Triton College, 1986b.

Mohr, L. "Triton College: In Two Decades the Vision Has Become a Reality." *Triton College Update*, Mar./Apr. 1984, pp. 2-9.

Nelson, R. (Assistant vice-chancellor for academic affairs, University of Illinois-Chicago.) Personal conversation with author, June 8, 1988.

Palmer, J. (Director of data collection and policy analysis, AACJC.) Telephone conversation with author, May 17, 1988.

Triton College Statistical Abstract 1987. River Grove, Ill.: Office of Research and Analysis, Triton College, 1987.

"Triton Encourages Persistence with Tuition Break." *Community, Technical, and Junior College Journal*, Aug./Sept. 1987, p. 43.

"Triton Ranked Number One in Corporate Support." *Proviso Star Sentinel*, May 4, 1988, p. 10.

Zwerling, L. S. "The Miami-Dade Story: Is It Really Number One?" *Change*, Jan./Feb. 1988, pp. 10-19.

Barbara K. Townsend is assistant professor of higher education at Loyola University of Chicago and is a former community college faculty member and administrator.

James L. Catanzaro is president of Triton College.

*This chapter offers an annotated bibliography of ERIC
documents and articles.*

Sources and Information: Discovering Institutional Strengths and Limitations

Glenda K. Childress

All colleges are not alike. A search for institutional distinctiveness can open up new opportunities for educators to learn about a community college's strengths and limitations. The first step in conducting such a search is to identify the processes that will afford valid, reliable information about distinctive characteristics—those empirical and perceived qualities that are valued by internal and external constituents.

Many documents in the ERIC data base will provide sources of information to assist in institutional self-assessments. The annotated bibliography that follows is divided into two sections: models and guidelines for institutional assessment, and examples of institutional self-studies. The first section offers methodologies for measuring a community college's quality and performance, as well as other characteristics, and includes frameworks for incorporating research findings into the college's mission. The latter section is comprised of reports that detail the process and results of self-studies undertaken by several community colleges.

Unless otherwise indicated, the ERIC documents listed in this bibliography are available in microfiche or paper copy from the ERIC Docu-

B. K. Townsend (ed.). *A Search for Institutional Distinctiveness.*
New Directions for Community Colleges, no. 65. San Francisco: Jossey-Bass, Spring 1989.

ment Reproduction Service (EDRS), 3900 Wheeler Avenue, Alexandria, VA 22304-6409 (1-800-227-3742). The microfiche price for documents under 481 pages is $0.82. Prices for paper copies are: 1-25 pages, $1.94; 25-50 pages, $3.88; for each additional 25 pages, add $1.94. These prices are subject to change. Postage must be added to all orders. The journal articles included in this bibliography are not available from EDRS and must be obtained through regular library channels.

Models and Guidelines for Institutional Assessment

Clarke de Toro, M. F. *A Design for Evaluation of the Institutional Goals of La Montana Regional College.* Puerto Rico: La Montana Regional College, 1984. 78 pp. (ED 253 292)

Describes the design of a system by which solid, empirical evidence of institutional goal achievement could be collected. The project report includes a discussion of the purpose and design of the project; a review of the literature on institutional goals and the appropriate means for measuring goal achievement; an enumeration of the goals of La Montana Regional College and the process measures to be applied; and a timetable for the design of outcome studies.

Findlen, G. L. *Program Review: A Model Community College Process and Instrument.* New Orleans, La.: Delgado Community College, 1987. 25 pp. (ED 276 483)

Provides an overview of the development of a program review process and instrument, and the subsequent validation of the process on three programs at Delgado Community College (DCC). Describes DCC's commitment to the development of a program review process as a means of enabling the college to respond more quickly to technological and economic changes. Appendices include a bibliography of materials on program review and DCC's program review documents.

Florida Community College. *Florida Community College at Jacksonville: Institutional Assessment.* Jacksonville: Florida Community College, 1987. 57 pp. (ED 293 585)

Looks at Florida Community College at Jacksonville's institutional assessment process. The report explains the role of institutional assessment in a cycle of planning, research, and marketing, and establishes the scope, purposes, and uses of the assessment. Of particular interest is an overview of scheduled in-depth reviews of all units and the preparation of reports on organizational strengths and weaknesses.

McLeod, M. W., and Carter, R. A. "The Measure of Quality in Two-Year Colleges." *Community College Review,* 1985-86, *13* (3), 14-20.

Details the methods and findings of a survey of current assessment practices in two-year colleges. Lists traditional quality measures and five approaches to assessing educational quality. Concludes that though many colleges are involved in formal quality assessment, there is limited agreement on definitions or measures of excellence.

Moore, K. M. (ed.). *Assessment of Institutional Effectiveness.* New Directions for Community Colleges, no. 52. San Francisco: Jossey-Bass, 1986.
Examines the context of the current intense interest in educational effectiveness. Presents basic steps in assessing institutional effectiveness (such as developing meaningful statements of institutional mission and goals, designing and implementing an institutional planning process, and identifying indicators of effectiveness). Discusses the current potential contributions of the institutional research components.

Stoodley, R. V., Jr. *An Approach to Postsecondary Accreditation with the Efficient Use of Human Resources and Cost Containment Methods.* Claremont: New Hampshire Vocational-Technical College, 1985. 27 pp. (ED 271 150)
Describes the single self-study method for both institutional and program accreditation that was developed and field-tested at New Hampshire Vocational-Technical College. The report details the process of conceptualizing, planning, and organizing the project, and provides the methods and format of the self-study model.

Thompson, C. P., Alfred, R. L., and Lowther, M. " 'Institutional Effort': A Reality-Based Model for Assessment of Community College Productivity." *Community College Review,* 1987, *15* (2), 28–37.
Presents a model for measuring community college effort (for example, current versus desired performance in the provision of programs, policies, and services) based on the content of college publications, workload policies and procedures, student and faculty perceptions of educational needs and existing programs, institutional support expenditures, and student-teacher ratios.

Townsend, B. K. "Past as Prologue: Seeds of an Institution's Identity." *Community, Junior, and Technical College Journal,* 1986, *57* (1), 46–49.
Provides guidelines for conducting research on a community college's past as a means of gaining insight about its institutional strengths and weaknesses and future directions. Suggests groups to interview and documents to analyze to construct the factual chronology and ways of seeking out campus lore and customs to enrich the history.

Yosemite Community College District. *Assessment Guide.* Modesto, Calif.: Yosemite Community College District, 1983. 76 pp. (ED 246 950)

Outlines an assessment process designed to provide an overall plan and structure for the ongoing review and updating of all undertakings in the Yosemite Community College District. An overview of the assessment process outlines its three major elements: the basic information system; periodic reviews conducted at the unit, college, and district levels; and the revisions and reallocations called for by the review process. Details the planning process at the unit and college level, covering mission, goals, and priorities and instructions for college-level review.

Zammuto, R. F., Krakower, J. Y., and Niwa, S. L. *Development of the Two-Year Version of the Institutional Performance Survey.* Boulder, Colo.: National Center for Higher Education Management Systems, 1985. 113 pp. (ED 269 086)

Describes the development and field testing of a two-year college version of the National Center for Higher Education Management System's (NCHEMS) Institutional Performance Survey (IPS), an instrument designed to provide information on the perceptions of various groups about the overall functioning and performance of the institution. Includes an extensive executive report on the field-testing portion of the study, presenting the responses of faculty and staff to questions related to changes in the college environment, enrollments, revenues, institutional functioning, college culture, institutional strategy, resource allocation, and institutional effectiveness.

Examples of Institutional Self-Studies

Barden, J. E. *Self-Study: Standing Rock Community College.* North Dakota: Standing Rock Community College, 1984. 114 pp. (ED 252 365)

Looks at a study conducted by the administration, faculty, staff, and other constituencies of Standing Rock Community College in preparation for its initial accreditation visit in April 1984. The purpose of the study was to provide complete descriptive information about the institution, focusing on the college's purpose, the people it serves, resources, management functions, instruction, and student/community services. The study report explores the steady growth of enrollment, efforts to improve efficiency in both facility care and student services, and short- and long-term goals for organizing college resources and achieving results.

College of Lake County. *Self Study, 1985: College of Lake County.* Grayslake, Ill.: College of Lake County, 1985. 160 pp. (ED 264 916)

This report represents a comprehensive self-analysis by the College of Lake County (CLC), which sought to involve the entire institution in an examination of CLC's mission, resources, accomplishments, and future plans. The purpose of the self-study is explored, as is the assessment and evaluation of programs and services, future directions related to the college's mission and institutional planning process, and the work of each committee involved in the self-study process and its conclusions.

GMA Research Corporation. *Community Colleges of Spokane Employee Survey*. Bellevue, Wa.: Spokane Community College, 1985. 51 pp. (ED 261 732)
Details a survey of Community Colleges of Spokane employees to identify the strengths and weaknesses of internal communications, to determine the colleges' image among its employees, to evaluate the colleges' delivery system, and to provide information regarding future directions. The survey instrument and results are appended.

Miami–Dade Community College. *Miami–Dade Community College 1984 Institutional Self-Study*. Vol. 7: *Mitchell Wolfson New World Center Campus Study (Evaluation of the Center for Business and Industry)*. Fla.: Miami–Dade Community College, 1985. 65 pp. (ED 259 775)
Part of a systematic, in-depth assessment of Miami-Dade Community College's (MDCC) educational programs, student support systems, and selected campus-level activities, this volume of the college's self-study report examines the impact and effectiveness of the Center for Business and Industry at MDCC's Wolfson Campus. Of particular interest is a section that describes the research design, which involved interviews and surveys to determine the perceptions of faculty, staff, administrators, and program participants; evaluation results and conclusions; and recommendations and implementation plans.

Morris, P., and Tuthill, S. *Internal Assessment as a First Step in Strategic Planning*. Wilmington: Delaware Technical and Community College, 1986. 25 pp. (ED 272 262)
Details the internal assessment process initiated at the Wilmington/Stanton Campus of Delaware Technical and Community College in preparation for a reaccreditation study and in response to a climate of rapid internal and external change. The purpose of the internal assessment is detailed; the roles played by the research team are described; the models used in the assessment design are explained; and samples of data collection instruments are provided, along with a discussion of steps in study design and implementation. The report concludes with an examination of the outcomes of the internal study, including the integration of strategic planning into organizational structure and the accreditation reaffirmation process.

Radcliffe, S. K., and Novak, V. E. *Howard Community College Staff Services Evaluation, Spring 1985.* Research report no. 41. Columbia, Md.: Office of Institutional Research, Howard Community College, 1985. 118 pp. (ED 256 455)

Describes a study conducted by Howard Community College to evaluate its provision of services during fiscal year 1985. The responses to a 153-item questionnaire of twenty-four faculty, thirty management team members, and thirty-eight support staff members are provided. The evaluation report includes tables showing, for each service area and questionnaire item, mean scores, number of respondents in each job category, frequency counts, and overall mean scores.

Steiner, S. *Genesee Community College Self-Study and Evaluation.* Paper presented at the Conference on Institutional Self-Assessment, Madison, N.J., March 16, 1983. 17 pp. (ED 258 622)

Provides a description of the self-study program review process developed by Genesee Community College (GCC) as an alternative to the traditional Middle States evaluation process. The paper examines the history of self-study at GCC from 1980; explores the roles and responsibilities of the Self-Study Steering Committee; lists the topics addressed in program self-studies (such as program history, goals, effectiveness measures, cohesiveness, and plans); and notes the importance of information sharing within the internal committee structure. The report also addresses the dissemination of self-study findings, and outlines the benefits and limitations of GCC's review process.

Weeks, R. G., Jr. *Challenges of Conducting a Self-Study Process: Small Two-Year Institutions.* Powell, Wy.: Northwest Community College, 1986. 198 pp. (ED 274 398)

Provides a description of the accreditation self-study process employed by Northwest Community College (NCC), along with a copy of the final self-study report that includes information on NCC's mission and goals, programs of instruction, students and student services, faculty, instructional support services, financial resources, physical facilities, community resources, and institutional dynamics. Information is presented on how the current college organizational structure was used to conduct the self-study, and the advantages for small colleges of using existing organizational structures rather than creating special self-study committees.

Glenda K. Childress is administrative coordinator at the ERIC Clearinghouse for Junior Colleges, University of California, Los Angeles.

Index

A

Academic accessibility, 4-5, 24
Academically oriented two-year colleges, 7, 25-26, 76-79, 83-86
Administrators, in community colleges, 61-62, 92; institutional evaluation and, 37, 42, 67-69; perceptions of, 26, 28-31, 93; at Triton College, 80-81, 82, 83, 85
Admission requirements, in four-year colleges, 5-6
Age of Reform, 50
Agriculture training, 18
Aims Community College, 14
Alaska, 13-14
Alaska Pacific Refining Company, 14
Alfred, R. L., 53, 56, 91
Alliss Opportunity Grant Program, 17
Alternative high school programs, 17
American Association of Community and Junior Colleges, 6, 9, 24, 32
American Association of University Professors, 12, 20
American Council of Life Insurance, 55
Anne Arundel Community College, 16
Arizona, 14, 19
Arkansas, 15
Ashland Community College, 15
Assessment, institutional. *See* Evaluation, institutional
Atlantic Monthly, 55
Automated manufacturing technology program, 18

B

Baker, G., III, 12, 21
Barden, J. E., 92
Bennett, W. J., 5, 10, 84, 87
Berquist, W. H., 77, 78, 87
Biofeedback Program, at Aims Community College, 14

Bismarck State College, 17-18, 20
Blackpool College, 16
Blocker, C. E., 12, 20
Board minutes, 51
Boatwright, J., 54, 56
Boucher, W. I., 54, 55, 56
Brawer, F. B., 76, 85, 87
Brick, M., 11, 13, 20
Brunton, D., 45-46, 56
Bunker Hill Community College, 16, 19
Butler County Community College, 20

C

California, 45
"Career Center of the Midwest," 77
Carter, R. A., 90-91
Catanzaro, J. L., 2, 73-88
Catawba Valley Technical College, 17
Cecil Community College, 16
Celebrating Two Decades of Innovation, 19, 21
Center for Business and Industry, 93
Center for Educational Statistics, 4, 10
Center of Emphasis, 18
Center for Study of Local Issues, 16
Central American Scholarship Program, 16
Central Arizona College, 14
Central Florida Community College, 14
Chandler, M. O., 21
Child-care training, 14-15
Childress, G. K., 89-94
City University of New York, 17
Clark, B. R., 12, 21, 67, 71
Clarke de Toro, M. F., 90
Cohen, A. M., 12, 21, 76, 85, 87
College committees, 35-42, 94
College of Lake County (CLC), 92-93
Colleges, four-year, 12-13, 24, 77-79; enrollment at, 4-6, 27, 61
Colleges of distinction, 9, 13-19
Colorado, 14

Fields, R. R., 11-12, 13, 21
Findlen, G. L., 90
Fisher, J. L., 62, 65
Flight Nursing Training, 14
Flight Paramedic Training, 14
Flight Respiratory Therapy training,
14
Florida, 9, 12, 14, 21, 90
Florida Association of Community
Colleges, 14, 21
Florida Community College, 90
Florida Department of Education, 14,
21
Florida Keys Community College, 14
Florida State Board of Community
Colleges, 14, 21
Flyde College, 16
Ford Motor Corporation, 78
Forest technician training, 14
France, 16
Frye, J., 84, 87
Fullerton Junior College (FJC), 45-
46, 56
Fullerton Union High School Dis-
trict, 45
Funding, in community colleges, 13,
24, 27-28, 70; programming and,
31, 32, 63; at Triton College, 73, 76,
83-84
Furniture industry training, 17

G

Garrett Community College, 16
Genesee Community College (GCC),
94
Geographic accessibility, 15, 24, 27-28
GMA Research Corporation, 93
Goldman, E. F., 50, 56
Goodwin, G., 19, 21
Gould, R. A., 77, 78, 87
Green Child, 47, 57
Greenberg, E. M., 77, 78, 87
Greenhouse operation and manage-
ment training, 77

H

Hagerstown Community College, 16
Handicapped training, 13
Hankin, J. N., 1, 11-21
Harford Community College, 16

Hawaii, 14-15, 19
"Hawaii No Ka Oi" program, 19
Haywood Community College, 19
Hazard Community College, 15
Health care training, 14, 15
Hebrew University, 18
High-technology training, 74, 84
Histories, institutional, 46, 49, 50-51,
55
Hofstader, R., 50, 56
Honolulu Community College, 14-15
Howard Community College, 94

I

Identity, institutional, 46-47, 49, 55-
56, 62, 64
Illinois, 15, 28, 73-89
Illinois Community College Board,
28, 73, 74, 76, 77, 85, 87
Illinois Public Community College
System, 73
Image, institutional, 1, 93; percep-
tions and, 6-9, 26-27, 32, 54, 62-65,
70, 71; at Triton College, 81, 86-87
Impact studies, institutional, 53, 55
Information gathering, 45-56
Innovation, 86, 87
Institutional Performance Survey
(IPS), 92
Integrity, institutional, 62, 63-64
Internal constituents, 89; institutional
evaluation and, 68, 69-71; percep-
tions of, 26-27, 28-32, 41; strategic
planning and, 54, 62, 63-64; at Tri-
ton College, 74-75, 79-83, 85-86, 87
Iowa, 15, 49-50, 52-53, 56
Israel, 18

J

Job Information Network, 16-17
Job-training, 14, 27, 53, 78, 79
Junior College Journal, 48

K

Kapiolani Community College, 19
Keller, G., 63-64, 65, 68, 72
Kellogg Community College, 16-17
Kellogg Foundation, 16, 20
Kentucky, 15, 20